PRINCE GEORGE'S COUNTY
AND THE
CIVIL WAR

Life on the Border

NATHANIA A. BRANCH MILES,
MONDAY M. MILES & RYAN J. QUICK

THE
History
PRESS

Published by The History Press
Charleston, SC 29403
www.historypress.net

First published 2013

Manufactured in the United States

ISBN 978.1.60949.848.1

Library of Congress CIP data applied for.

Contents

Acknowledgements

Although this book was a collaborative effort by us, the coauthors, we could not have completed it without the help of many others, whom we feel deserve to be credited for their contributions. First and foremost, we must thank all of our family and friends who have provided moral support, motivation and encouragement throughout the entire process, especially Nicole Miles, Matt Johnson, Richard Quick and Rosalind Ubiles. Our most important supporter was Imara Ashton Miles, who assisted with the research in data collection, scanning and copying documents of vital importance to the book. Imara is a budding family historian and genealogist and has developed great research skills.

We definitely could not have even begun this project without the people who pointed us in the right direction during our research. Another important supporter was Susan Pearl, a historian and volunteer at the Frederick S. DeMarr Library at the Greenbelt Branch Library. Susan provided a wealth of information and sources regarding Prince George's County during the Civil War and also helped with editing and proofreading chapters. A special thanks to the wonderful ladies at the University of Maryland at College Park Special Collections Library—Elizabeth A. Novara, curator of historical manuscripts; Anne Turkos, university archivist; and Malissa Ruffer, researcher—for their guidance and expertise on the Maryland Agricultural College and the Rossborough Inn during the Civil War. Laurie Verge, historian and director of the Surratt House Museum, was equally valuable in providing information and also helped guide us to interesting stories and topics. Joan Chaconas, history specialist at the Surratt House Museum, provided us with some of the photos we have included in this book. Aaron Macovitch with the Anacostia Heritage Trails of Maryland also helped us find photos and information. We thank John Peter Thompson, chairman of the Prince George's County Historic Preservation Commission, for his insight into the life of Dr. John H. Bayne. We are especially thankful to everyone who helped us collect photos, which were not nearly as easy to find as we anticipated.

We would also like to thank Jane Taylor Thomas, who assisted with reading and editing chapters; Dr. Ann Wass, historian/museum specialist, and Ms. Ferris at the Riversdale House Museum; Sandra Walia, research librarian at the Surratt Museum's James O. Hall Research Center; and Francis O' Neill, senior research librarian at the Maryland Historical Society Museum.

Lastly, we would like to thank the librarians at the Hyattsville Library, Maryland Historical Society Library and the Enoch Pratt Library who pointed us to sources that helped us tell these very important stories that are a major part of our county's history.

Introduction

Depending on whom you ask, the American Civil War between the Northern and Southern states was fought over the issue of slavery or states' rights. Perhaps it was a little of both. Either way, when the Confederate soldiers fired on the Union soldiers at Fort Sumter, South Carolina, on April 12, 1861, Americans on both sides believed the war would be quick, lasting only a couple weeks. Following the call for volunteers, thousands of men joined the two armies to fight the good fight. The men who volunteered to fight in the Northern and Southern armies were young and old, black and white. Soon, there were neighbors fighting neighbors and brothers fighting brothers over ideology and loyalty. Instead of the quick war envisioned by many, the war lasted from 1861 to 1865 and led to causalities of approximately 618,000 on both sides. No one dreamed that the war would last as long as it did, nor did anyone consider the heavy costs of war as it related to human life and the economy. During the Civil War, Maryland was a border state and did not secede from the Union. Nonetheless, while not a part of the Confederacy, Maryland soon found itself occupied by Federal forces. In the words of President Abraham Lincoln, the Federal City would not survive the war if it were surrounded by enemies on all sides, hence the border states would have to remain neutral.

The specific reasons for the War Between the States may vary among scholars, but the dispute between the North and the South can be linked to (1) the economic and social differences between the regions, (2) the question of states' rights versus federal rights, (3) the fight between slave and non-slave state proponents to maintain or fight the spread of slavery to U.S. territories, (4) the growth of the abolitionist movement and (5) the election of Abraham Lincoln in 1860. The aforementioned reasons caused a young nation of thirty-six states to divide into two separate camps, with the border states separating the two. The Confederate States of America included South Carolina, Mississippi, Florida, Alabama, Georgia, Louisiana, Texas, Virginia, Arkansas, Tennessee and North Carolina. The Northern states that remained in the Union were California, Connecticut, Delaware, Illinois, Indiana, Iowa, Kansas, Kentucky, Maine, Maryland, Massachusetts, Michigan, Minnesota, Missouri, Nevada, New Hampshire, New Jersey, New York, Ohio, Oregon, Pennsylvania, Rhode Island, Vermont, West Virginia and Wisconsin. The border states of Kentucky, Delaware, Missouri and Maryland did not secede for reasons of their own, but at the same time, they were not completely loyal to the Union. Due to the geographic location of Maryland, it was difficult to openly take a side. Although Washington, D.C., was not a state, it remained a slaveholding territory within the Union.

Maryland's demographics divided the state into three geographical regions. Of Maryland's residents, 60 percent lived in northern Maryland, which included Allegany, Baltimore, Carroll, Frederick, Hartford and Washington Counties, whose primary economies were dairy and agriculture. Southern Maryland accounted for less than 19 percent of the population, but the majority of the slaveholders and their slaves resided in Anne Arundel, Calvert, Charles, Montgomery, Prince George's and St. Mary's Counties. The remaining 22 percent of the state's population occupied the Eastern Shore, which included Caroline, Cecil, Dorchester, Kent, Queen Anne's, Somerset, Talbot and Worchester Counties. By 1850, 70 percent of Maryland's white population resided in northern Maryland. Many Irish and German immigrants settled in northern Maryland, particularly in Baltimore, and white residents were leaving southern Maryland and the Eastern Shore for job opportunities and wealth. Between 1820 and 1850, 130,000 immigrants arrived in Baltimore and went on to work the harbor and farms. By 1860, Baltimore held 68 percent of Maryland's foreign-born population. Baltimore played a major role in Maryland's economic growth and industrial progression; its location as the southernmost of the major ports gave it an advantage in the West Indian trade as a whole.

Prior to the start of the war, Montgomery and Prince George's Counties, as well as counties in Virginia, donated land to create the federal city of Washington, D.C. This change in the landscape caused the two counties to lie clearly on the border connecting them on three sides to the north and south through the Baltimore & Ohio Railroad. While there were no major battles or skirmishes in Prince George's County during the war, it was essential that the county remain in the Union because of its proximity to Washington, D.C. During the war, there were no natural boundaries between the District of Columbia and Prince George's County, and the roads between the two were heavily guarded at all times. The Federal government commissioned at least two forts to be built in Prince George's County during the war: Fort Foote was built to defend the capital of Washington, D.C., while Fort Lincoln was constructed near the District line in Bladensburg. The communities of Bladensburg, Vansville, Beltsville, Good Luck, Long Old Fields (Forestville), Upper Marlborough and Queen Anne (ghost town) were involved in the war through indirect citizen participation.

In the immediate years preceding the Civil War, Maryland was torn between two worlds that stood in stark contrast with each other: the industrial North and the agricultural South. In the words of historian Barbara Fields, there were "two Maryland's…one funded upon slavery and the other on open free labor.[1] Nowhere in the state of Maryland was this more apparent than in Prince George's County. Created by an act of the Maryland General Assembly on April 23, 1696, Prince George's County was formed from land that previously belonged to both Charles and Calvert Counties. When the war first started, Prince George's County was one of the richest and most productive plantation counties in Maryland. Tobacco was the main crop of Maryland's southern plantations, but the crop had a labor-intensive process and could not operate at the full efficiency without the benefit of slave labor. Early on during the county's history, farm owners realized that they could not afford to keep their farms afloat just with the labor of indentured servants, who were able to run away and blend into society without completing their service. As a county totally dependent on the free labor of slaves, Prince George's County could not support the abolition of slavery, much less free them or pay them. The work was too much, and the white men would not be able to work under the harsh conditions and long hours needed to produce the tobacco, corn and other products of the field.

While the gentry of Prince George's County were both conservative and sympathetic toward their Southern brethren, many did not want to take the radical step of seceding from the Union; however, others in the county called for secession and served the Confederacy as soldiers or spies. The *Planter's Advocate*, a newspaper serving Prince George's County, complained that the "least exertion on the part of the friends of the movement could have elicited a vote that would have overwhelmed the opposition," but the

Map of Prince George's County showing District 3, Upper Marlborough.
Library of Congress, Prints and Photographs Division.

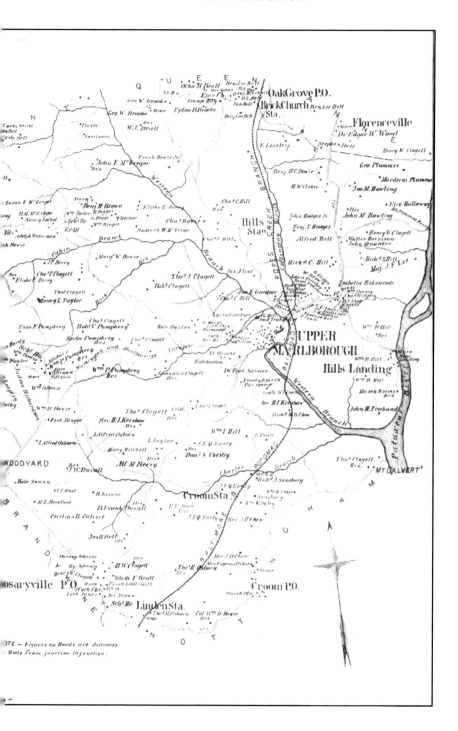

complaint was too late. As long as they were in the business of growing and selling tobacco, many Prince Georgians needed the continuation of a labor system that would guarantee them laborers for a lifetime, hence their decision to defend the institution of slavery.

As long as slavery was not threatened, Maryland would not move to secede. During the first year of the war, the Federal government made it clear that Maryland and other border states could keep their slaves if they would remain in the Union. To Marylanders fighting to stay in the Union, by this move, the Federal government was essentially saying that the war against the South was a war against rebellion and not slavery. Prince Georgians would not have to fight against the South if they did not want to. There was no draft in the first year of the war, and even after the government started a draft system, substitutes could be found elsewhere in the state to go in the draftee's place.

The voices of Maryland's people clearly illustrated a divided populace reflecting the state's tortured status as a border state participating in a war that pitted the South against the North and caused turmoil between fathers, sons and brothers. The free state of Maryland was literally caught between a rock and hard place because of its proximity to Washington, D.C. In his wisdom, President Lincoln realized that the Union could ill afford for Maryland to follow Virginia and secede from the Union. As a result, Maryland was saved for the Union whether it liked it or not. Maryland was so much like its Southern counterparts that Virginia had difficulty understanding why the state did not secede. As the war came to a close, and Confederate general Robert E. Lee surrendered to Union general Ulysses Grant at Appatomox Court House, the former slaves of the South and Prince George's County found themselves free from bondage and trying to acclimate themselves in a new world. The plantation owners found themselves left with ruined farms and no labor force. The economy and infrastructure of Prince George's County lay in ruins. The county, which in 1860 produced 13 million pounds of tobacco, produced only 4 million pounds by 1870. The conclusion of the Civil War brought the end of "Old Prince George's County," and instead of a plantation economy, a new economy of small farms, quaint country villages and modest living became the norm.

Chapter 1

Living on the Border

According to Kurt Detwiller, Maryland in the 1850s was a microcosm of America. The divergent forces of slavery and the free market came together with industrialization and agriculture. Even though slavery remained strong in the southern counties and on the Eastern Shore, the northern and western parts of the state never fully embraced slavery. Baltimore, while politically pro Southern, had strong economic ties with the industrial North. Baltimore also had the fastest growing free population in the United States.[2] As a border state, Maryland's sympathies were culturally, geographically and economically tied to the South, and yet many of its citizens were hesitant to leave the Union when many of its sister states, especially Virginia, seceded. With the outbreak of war, President Lincoln and his administration viewed the boundary lines that separated Maryland and Washington, D.C., with great trepidation, questioning Maryland's loyalty to both the North and South. Answering the call to arms, many men left their homes to fight for either the Confederate or Union cause. As of 1863, there were approximately 18,000 men from Maryland serving in the Confederate army and 53,000 serving in the Union army. Anticipating a short and quick war, many Prince George's County citizens faced illness, injuries and death while at war. The war also had repercussions for those left behind, as the families struggled to survive on dwindling resources as well as trying to maintain the family homestead. The Civil War drained manpower from Maryland farms as men—both black and white—joined Northern and Southern armies. In southern Maryland, particularly in

Prince George's County, a substantial portion of the agricultural work force—black slaves—sought freedom by either running away or joining the Union army. It is estimated that 100,000 slaves valued at some $50 million were lost from Maryland during the Civil War.

In Maryland, the southern counties had a unique blend of Southern agrarianism, while the northern and western counties leaned toward mercantilism. In addition, the western and northern portions of the state were shifting demographically as new immigrants began arriving from Germany and Ireland. For these new immigrants, who had no need for slave labor, the furor over slavery was a moot point. Unlike the new immigrants, those Marylanders who lived in the southern counties and on the Eastern Shore relied heavily on slavery. The economy of Prince George's County was based largely on the growth of such crops as tobacco, corn and vegetables, as well as the free labor of slaves.

When the Civil War began, the residents of Prince George's County found themselves in the middle of a war zone threatened by both Union and Confederate forces. The Federal city of Washington, D.C., bordered Maryland on the western, eastern and northern sides of the county. Across the Potomac River lay the Confederate state of Virginia. The road between Prince George's County and Washington, D.C., was heavily guarded by Union troops. And while no actual skirmishes or battles were fought in Prince George's County, the threat of a battle taking place in the county was a legitimate fear for many residents, with the Confederate army constantly on the move and the visible presence of the Union army in the state. The Union army guarded the Baltimore & Ohio rail lines in Bladensburg, Maryland; marched throughout the countryside; and monitored the Federal forts along the Potomac River around Washington, D.C.

Prince Georgians who were Confederate sympathizers—as well as anyone suspected of associating with known spies—were subjected to raids that included the confiscation or destruction of their personal property, including supplies, animals and food, and potentially becoming a Union prisoner. In July 1864, Confederate general Jubal Early commanded the last Confederate invasion of Maryland when he dispatched four hundred cavalrymen under Maryland native and Confederate general Bradley Tyler Johnson. General Johnson cut the rail communications north of Baltimore and between Baltimore and Washington. On July 11, the Confederate army blew up the rail line in Beltsville, Maryland, and cut the telegraph wires. During their stay in Maryland, in retaliation for the Union forces burning the home of Virginia governor John Letcher, the Confederate army proceeded to burn the home of Maryland governor Augustus Bradford. The Confederate army spent the next night at the Maryland Agricultural College. The Rossborough Inn was turned over to General Johnson and served as the Confederate headquarters until the troops were prepared to move on toward Montgomery County en route to Pennsylvania. The Confederate army also demanded that the towns of Hagerstown and Frederick pay a ransom to avoid their towns being burned.

SOUTHERN SYMPATHIES

While some of the residents of Prince George's County wanted to preserve the peace and harmony of the Union, there were many residents who supported the South and understood the need for secession following the election of Abraham Lincoln. The question of expanding slavery into the new territories caused great tensions between those in the South, who supported slavery, and those in the North, whose economy was not dependent on it. Slavery was a hot topic among those in the South. Southern sympathizers felt that the right to own slaves was a right given to slave owners via the U.S. Constitution, and they would make no effort to stop the spread of slavery or apologize for the institution of slavery. The typical Southerner could not understand why the North was so against the practice. In southern Maryland and the Eastern Shore, the plantation regions, the issue of slavery was a very sensitive one, and emphasis was placed on Northern wrongs and Southern grievances. Unionist expressions in these areas were more qualified and predisposed toward a Southern position. The Southern states also failed to acknowledge the impact the Industrial Revolution had over the agriculture economy, which was dependent on cotton, tobacco and, most importantly, the free labor provided by the slaves.

Many Americans who supported slavery feared that the election of Abraham Lincoln in 1860 would result in the end of slavery not just in future territories but in the current states as well. Following Lincoln's election but prior to his inauguration, these concerns resulted in the Southern states seceding and founding the Confederate States of America in February 1861. Sharing a common heritage forged by the "peculiar institution of Slavery," a large segment of Marylanders had strong sympathies for the South and expressed a desire for Maryland to secede as well. Nonetheless, the state was both strongly conflicted and attached to the Union, which explains why, when the special session of the Maryland General Assembly met in Frederick, Maryland, to decide on the issue of secession, the vote to secede was not unanimous. Preferring a compromise, Maryland remained indecisive during the early days of the war, and it was not until 1861 that Maryland's adherence to the Union was firmly settled beyond doubt. For President Lincoln, Maryland's geographical position in surrounding the capital and in controlling the rail lines to Washington made the state's continued loyalty essential. The Union soldiers' presence and Federal intervention into state affairs ended all real ability of Marylanders to make any other decision.

LEFT BEHIND AT HOME

For many in Prince George's County, the war was especially hard, as many families had strong blood ties and relationships with those who were on the opposite side of the conflict. The war also placed an economic burden on many families. As the husband or the eldest son was often the primary breadwinner of the family, the family suffered financially when they went off to war. The women, children and old men who were left behind also suffered greatly from the raids on their farms by soldiers who often stole food, money and animals because they felt that their need was greater than the family's. Those left behind had to deal with food shortages, as well as price increases; what had cost $1.00 in 1860 cost $1.82 in 1864.[3]

Women living in southern Maryland near the border were continuously confronted by the challenges of dealing with the Union army or being in charge of the home for the first time. Southern gentlewomen, particularly those of the affluent landowners, did not want to lose their previous status as lady of the manor, but the war took its toll on everyone south of the Mason-Dixon line. War did not discriminate, so there were difficult adjustments for women who were either brides one day and widows the next or ladies of the manor who previously had no working knowledge of the family farm but were now in charge of the day-to-day running of the homestead. The women who were left to take care of the homefront had to develop survival skills so that they could keep their farms operating and maintain the existing slave workforce. Many of these slaves used the

Civil War envelope with the message "Liberty and Union." *Library of Congress, Prints and Photographs Division.*

chaos created by the war to either runaway from the plantations or join the Union army. While many women were dependent on their slaves to do most of the work and keep the farm operating, this did not stop the women from volunteering their services in making bandages, writing letters to the wives and families of the wounded soldiers or occasionally becoming spies themselves and sharing vital information to whichever side they supported. Life was especially difficult for the women who became widows when their husbands died in battle or from disease far away from home.

FIRST FAMILIES OF PRINCE GEORGE'S COUNTY

There were many Prince Georgians who were not happy with the election of President Lincoln and the subsequent secession. This was especially true among the county's upper class. As a result, many men of these affluent first families of Prince George's County showed their loyalty to the cause by slipping across the Potomac to join the Confederate army. However, there were just as many Prince Georgians who decided to fight for the Union cause. Brothers, fathers and sons of Prince George's

The home of slaveholder Bennett Gwynn suffered a midnight raid by the Federal government but was burned by an unknown slave. *Library of Congress, Prints and Photographs Division.*

County found themselves openly fighting one another on opposite sides of the battlefield, and a few worked as spies for one side or the other. As a result, many plantations and private homes were subjected to frequent raids by the Federal forces searching for weapons and supplies intended for shipments going south. These random raids left many families destitute and homeless. Some of the poorer families became refugees of war. Many homes were destroyed and livestock killed and/or stolen by both Union and Confederate forces. There was also the fear of guilt by association, for the family members of those who were considered disloyal to the Union also faced the possibility of being arrested by Union forces whether or not they shared the same views.

Many families in Prince George's County experienced tragedies as a result of the Civil War. The home of Bennett Gwynn was set on fire by a disgruntled slave. When Lieutenant Colonel John Waring was arrested for treason, his plantation home in Upper Marlboro, named the Bald Eagle, was confiscated by the Union army. His wife and daughters were subsequently arrested. There were also families who suffered the loss of a loved one, including the Bowie and the Bryan families, both of whom suffered the death of a son as a result of the war.

The Economy of Prince George's County

The economy of Prince George's County was based overwhelmingly on agriculture and provided great wealth to landowners both large and small. Per the Eighth Census of the United States, Prince George's County had the largest population of slaves in the state of Maryland. The affluent class, which included the county's slave-owning families, led the social and public standard of living in a manner befitting the time. By 1860, the county was producing more than 13 million pounds of tobacco annually for shipment to the North and Europe. In addition, the area also produced 300,000 bushels of wheat and about 700,000 bushels of corn, and local farmers owned 5,000 horses, 4,000 milk cows, 9,000 sheep and 2,500 swine. Much, if not all, of the work was done by slaves; among the 2,000 white families in the county, there were 850 slaveholders holding 12,500 black men, women and children in bondage.

While Prince George's County's agricultural crops included corn and wheat, the main crop was tobacco, and that is the primary reason the county was dependent on the free labor of slavery. As a result, the slaveholding families of Prince George's County were in favor of fighting for the right of the state to dictate whether slavery would be allowed there. The war was hard on the men, women and children, regardless of which side they supported. Despite the fact that a majority of the war was fought in the South, the war had a direct impact on the economies of both the United States of America and the Confederate States of America. When the men left home to support the war, the women were left to pick up the slack and keep the home fires burning. War also had a profound effect on the changing role of women. Although women were used to working on the family farms, many found that their workload increased as a result of the men in their family going off to war. For the women of the affluent class who had no idea how to run their farms without the benefit of their men folk or slaves, it was a new and challenging experience. When the war first began, many in both the North and South were of the opinion that it would be over fairly quickly. Instead, many found themselves struggling to remain steadfast as the war entered its fourth year. Young men on both sides were dying quickly, and those who came home did so to die or were maimed so severely that they could no longer participate in helping with the day-to-day running of the farm. As a result of the war, many families were forced into bankruptcy or lost their farms.

Despite the misconception that Prince George's County was the home to many large landowners and slaveholders, a majority of the working farms and/or plantations in Prince George's County had a minimum of one to six slaves. Most were producers of tobacco, a very labor-intensive crop, and were dependent on free labor. These affluent farmers lived in an agrarian society where they made their living growing tobacco, grain and dairy products.

In 1861, when the state was still pondering whether to secede or stay in the Union, Prince George's County sent four elected representatives to a special session of the General Assembly in Annapolis. These representatives—Edward Pilny Bryan, Ethan A. Jones, Richard Wooten and John Brooke—were plantation owners and slaveholders who were in favor of secession and voted accordingly. In the session, Bryan presented a petition from the voters of Prince George's County asking for a vote on secession; he later protested the assembly's lack of action. When it became evident that Maryland would not secede from the Union, scores of young men left their homes and the county to join the fight for the Confederacy. Many Prince Georgians who were Southern sympathizers made supreme sacrifices in terms of life and property.

Dr. John H. Bayne, an influential slaveholder and practicing physician, represented Prince George's County as state senator from 1861 to 1865. A civic-minded man, Dr. Bayne also served his community as a justice of the peace and worked with Charles B. Calvert in the development

Salubria, home of Maryland state senator Dr. John H. Bayne, horticulturist and advocate for fellow slaveholders in Prince George's County. *Library of Congress, Prints and Photographs Division.*

and implementation of the Maryland Agricultural College. A respected horticulturist, Dr. Bayne was known to have over five thousand fruit trees, which included strawberries and tomatoes as well as eight hundred peach trees. Dr. Bayne was the proud owner of the Salubria plantation in the Spalding's District (now known as Oxon Hill), where he and his young family resided and had approximately seventy slaves. As a senator, Dr. Bayne was an advocate for all Maryland slaveholders who had witnessed their property flee to the capital city. During the war, Dr. Bayne was in constant communication with Maryland governors Hicks and Bradford and attempted to work with the White House regarding the issue of runaway slaves seeking Federal assistance in their return. Prior to the Civil War, Dr. Bayne had rarely manumitted any of his slaves; however, he did release members of the Hatton family from his servitude. In the waning days of the war, unable to stop the self-emancipation of his slaves, Dr. Bayne slowly reconciled himself to the end of slavery. During the Constitutional Convention of 1864, his support of the abolition of slavery contributed to the passage of the legislation.

The Bowie family was another influential family who had large plantations in Prince George's County and Virginia. The family owned thousands of acres and more than seventy slaves in the county. This Prince Georgian family also had unlimited political clout, including having several key politicians and governors in their ancestry. The Bowies intermarried with other prominent families such as Snowden, Magruder, Plummer, Calvert, Clagett and Addison. This often led to the acquisition of more land, which was merged with the Bowie land to create larger plantations. The Bowie family was a typical pro-Southern Prince George's family, and its support of the Southern cause led Walter "Wat" Bowie, son of Adeline (Snowden) and Walter W. Bowie, to enlist as an officer in the Confederate army and as a captain in Mosby's Rangers. Walter was a trained lawyer practicing his trade in Upper Marlboro when war was declared. When Maryland voted not to secede from the Union, Wat left Prince George's County and went to Richmond, Virginia, where he joined the Confederate army as an officer. Wat was extremely useful to the Confederacy, as he was very familiar with the roads in and out of the Federal City, Montgomery County and Prince George's County. Wat Bowie was a resourceful but sometimes reckless man, and he returned to the county several times, both to gather information and to visit his family. Captain Bowie was captured once and imprisoned but escaped before he could be executed. While visiting his relatives (the family of

Home of Governor Oden Bowie, slaveholder and relative of Walter Bowie. *Library of Congress, Prints and Photographs Division.*

John Waring), he escaped capture by disguising himself as a slave woman and brazenly walked past Union soldiers searching the property. Wat's luck finally ran out in 1864, when he and his men raided a store owned by Quakers in Montgomery County in the town of Sandy Spring. Little did Wat and his compatriots know that the farmers were very tired of the military destroying their property and stealing their livestock. After the storeowners altered the nearby Union forces, Wat was mortally wounded when he tried to escape their clutches and died a few hours later. His brother Brune stayed with him until he died, at which point he was also captured by the Union. Captain Walter Bowie was buried at the family home, Willow Grove, near Holy Trinity Church in Collington. He was twenty-seven years old.

Adam Francis Plummer was a slave who lived and worked at the Riversdale Plantation. Adam and his family were owned by the well-known and aristocratic Calvert family, who also owned more than seventy other slaves working on their many properties. Adam was one of George Benedict Calvert's most trusted slaves and as such was granted many liberties. Even though George owned Adam, they had played together as children and forged a lifetime friendship that led to Adam becoming foreman of the Riversdale Plantation in 1864. George had set aside provisional grounds that allowed Adam to cultivate crops during his "free time" to supplement the meager rations he was given as a slave. He also sold his crops at the market. On May 30, 1841, Adam Francis Plummer, son of Barney and Sarah (Norris) Plummer, married Emily Saunders, daughter of Nellie (Beckett) and William Norris, at the New York Avenue Presbyterian Church in Washington, D.C. The ceremony included an official certificate of marriage, an honor rarely bestowed on slaves and most likely the

Adam Plummer, former slave of Charles B. Calvert. *Courtesy of Smithsonian Anacostia Community Museum.*

result of Adam's connection to the Calvert family. Emily Saunders was of mixed parentage; her mother was an English indentured servant and her father a black slave. Initially, Adam and Emily Plummer were permitted to see each other only on the weekends, when Adam would walk eight miles to visit Emily from Saturday evening until Monday. During the course of twenty-two years, Adam and Emily would have nine children: Sarah Miranda, Elias Quincy, Henry Vinton, Julia Caroline, Nicholas Saunders, Marjory Ellen Rose, Margaret and twins Robert Francis and Nellie Arnold.

As with other slave families prior to the war, there was always the danger of being sold at any time without notice or reason. Slavery divided many black families in Maryland, and Adam and his wife were an example of how slavery divided the Plummer family. On December 22, 1855, Adam's wife and five of their children were sold in an auction to Gilbert Thompson. The new owner of Adam's wife and children lived in a mansion on Meridian Hill in Washington, D.C., fifteen miles from the Calvert plantation in Riversdale. Emily Saunders Plummer would later be sold to another plantation, Mount Hebron, which was located in Howard County, twenty miles southwest of Baltimore. Adam and Sarah were married for twenty-two years before they finally lived under one roof. Before Emily was sold, Adam remained at the Riversdale plantation, while Emily Saunders Plummer lived on a plantation called Three Sisters, located in Lanham, Maryland.

When Charles Calvert died on May 24, 1864, he freed all the slaves who hadn't run away to Washington, D.C., or joined the Union army. Included in the freed slaves were many of Adam's brothers and sisters, who then relocated to Arlington, Virginia, and southwest Washington. In 1868, Adam Francis Plummer purchased ten acres of land near Riversdale for $1,000. In 1870, he finished building the family's first home, where they were able to live together at last.

As a direct descendant of Lord Baltimore, Charles B. Calvert was the seventh great-grandson of the founder of the colony of Maryland and a relative of six Maryland governors. The family owned more than 1,900 acres stretching along the Baltimore-Washington Turnpike, which is now Route 1 along the Capital Beltway. Charles grew up at Riversdale, constantly

The Riversdale home of Charles B. Calvert. *Library of Congress, Prints and Photograph Division.*

experimenting with new crops, animal breeds, irrigation, fertilizers and new farm machinery. Although Charles was a slaveholder, he was known to have mixed feelings about slavery. When his father died, he freed fifty slaves, and as the war proceeded, he freed them all. Charles never publicly denounced slavery, but it was known that his father had a slave mistress and that he took care of his half brothers and sisters who were born into slavery and then quietly freed them.

Colonel John Henry Waring and his family were well-known Southern sympathizers who owned more than 1,300 acres on a plantation originally known as Marsham's Rest. The plantation, which was located along the Patuxent River south of Nottingham, had been in the Waring family for more than 250 years. When it was discovered that two of Waring's eldest sons had entered the Confederate army and that he had been visited by Captain Walter Bowie, Federal authorities in Washington, D.C., ordered his arrest. In addition, the Waring family home was confiscated by the Union army. According to the journal of Julia Victoria Waring, Robert Bowie Waring died on December 28, 1863, from typhoid fever at Strausburg, and William Worthington Waring, who was seventeen, was very ill. The event that triggered the seizure of the family home was the May 1863 visit of Walter "Wat" Bowie, who escaped with the help of Julia's older sister, Elizabeth Margaret. In order to disguise Wat from the Union soldiers, Elizabeth Margaret colored Wat's face and hands with soot and dressed him as a slave

Lieutenant Colonel John Waring, slaveholder and CSA officer, was a cousin of Walter "Wat" Bowie, whose property was confiscated by the Federal government and whose family was jailed for treason. *Courtesy of University of Maryland Archives.*

woman. Colonel Waring was away during this visit, but upon his return, he learned that his family had been arrested. The women were taken to the Willard Hotel and placed under guard. Colonel Waring and Elizabeth were imprisoned at the Old Capitol Prison. Elizabeth remained at the prison for one month and learned that her brother William was in danger of being shot or hanged, as he had been tried and convicted as a spy. Elizabeth attempted to get a pardon for her brother through President Lincoln, but the officer in charge refused to acknowledge the pardon, tearing up the note and refusing her request to go to Fort Delaware. Eventually, William was sent to Point Lookout, where he exchanged identification with another prisoner and made his way back into the Confederate army.

John Wilkes Booth, a native of Baltimore, was a Southern sympathizer whose hatred of President Abraham Lincoln was well known. A frequent

visitor to Prince George's County, Booth was often seen visiting the Surrattsville tavern and having conversations with people like Dr. Samuel Mudd, David Herold, Mary Surratt, John Surratt Jr. and other known Confederate sympathizers. Booth's mere association with some of the families of Prince George's County greatly affected their lives and changed their destinies.

The Surratt family was another distinguished family from an old line in Maryland. A farmer and slaveholder who also owned various parcels of property throughout the county, John Surratt Sr. had inherited both the land and slaves from his parents. He owned as many as six slaves and often rented them out

Mary Surratt, the first woman executed by the United States government. *Courtesy of the Surratt House Museum.*

during hard financial times. In 1840, John married Mary Eugenia Jenkins of Waterloo, Maryland, who bore him two sons, Isaac and John Jr., and a daughter, Anna. As a tavern owner, John was appointed postmaster, and the community became known as Surrattsville, although it later adopted its current name of Clinton. As soon as war was declared, John's eldest son, Isaac, signed up with a Maryland Confederate group in Virginia while John Jr. worked behind the scenes with other known conspirators as a spy. After the death of John Sr., John Jr. assumed the position as postmaster until he was dismissed for suspicious behavior. Through their affiliation with John Wilkes Booth, the family would later become infamous for their support of the Confederacy as well as their

Dr. Samuel Mudd, slaveholder, known Southern sympathizer and conspirator with John Wilkes Booth in the assassination of President Lincoln. *Library of Congress, Prints and Photographs Division.*

alleged role in the assassination of President Lincoln. Following Lincoln's assassination, John Jr. escaped to Canada. Unfortunately, his mother, Mary, would become the first woman executed by the U.S. government for the assassination of the president. His sister Anna was an admirer of the actor John Wilkes Booth until the trial of her mother and fellow conspirators. She lived a distraught life full of mental delusions before dying in 1904. John would eventually return to the States, where he would live to the ripe old age of seventy-two.

Another Prince George's family who experienced loss during the war were the Lanhams, who resided near the railroad. The Lanhams made a moderate living working as planters cultivating tobacco, dairy and vegetables on their farms. As with other families who sympathized with the Confederacy, their greatest sacrifice was that of their young men—the

Benjamin Lewis Lanham of Prince George's County joined the CSA and died at age nineteen from injuries suffered in the war. *Private collection of Paul T. Lanham.*

brothers, sons and fathers who fought to save their way of life. Benjamin Lewis Lanham (1844–1863), son of Trueman and Mary Ellen Lanham, was one of the many young men who went south, joining the First Maryland Battalion, CSA, later known as the Second Maryland Infantry. Young Benjamin Lanham was killed at Gettysburg, Pennsylvania, during the assault on Culp's Hill, just one month shy of his nineteenth birthday.

The Civil War in Maryland, especially in Prince George's County, had a lot of Southern sympathizers who supported states' rights and the institution of slavery. Regrettably, they underestimated the cost of the war in terms of human life and property. The romance of war faded as young men died in battle or from disease. Women contributed to the war effort as spies, nurses, cooks, laundresses, supporters, organizers and mourners. The women and children who were left behind did their share in keeping the home fires burning, maintaining the land, helping out the soldiers at the hospitals or following their husbands into the war. Families were faced with new hardships they never would have considered before the war. During the war, Prince Georgians suffered many losses: the loss of property (e.g. land, livestock and slaves); the loss of their beautiful antebellum homes that were destroyed as a result of looting, raising and burning; and the loss of their men, who died as a result of the war. Fortunes based on the plantation economy were completely bankrupted, and families were fractured. Slave owners, including Dr. John Bayne, tried to secure compensation for those who had lost their property as a result of the war. But even the discussed amount would not be adequate compensation. The devastated families who survived the war could see only a bleak future in which it would take an incredibly long time to rebuild (if rebuilding was even possible). Even a returning solider was the not the same man who had left happy to go to war. When the war was over, the lifestyles of many were changed forever, and Prince George's County and its residents began to live life in a new economy based on wage labor.

Chapter 2

Maryland Agricultural College

A group of wealthy Maryland planters who belonged to the affluent Baltimore Farmer's Club organized and founded a private educational institution in 1848. Known as the Maryland Agricultural College (MAC), the school was designed for agricultural studies on crop diversification, fertilizers, horticulture innovations, animal husbandry and new research on agricultural technologies. The aim was to create an agricultural research college where the wealthy landowners and their sons could learn how to effectively manage, operate and maintain their lands, farms and slaves. The movement for the college came from the large plantation owners and was both generous and self-serving, as they wanted to educate only their own sons and the sons of their well-off neighbors.

Charles Benedict Calvert, a direct descendant of the founders of Maryland, the Lord Baltimores, was a relative of six Maryland governors and a future U.S. congressman.[4] Charles, who had been educated in private schools and attended the University of Virginia, envisioned an agricultural institution to teach modern agricultural practices such as crop rotation, artificial grasses, Hawthorn hedges and blooded stock in his home state. Dr. John H. Bayne, a Maryland state senator known for his own agricultural research, was also a visionary in the design and planning of this agricultural wonder.

The Baltimore Farmer's Club members, considered to be the "intelligent farmers," were the wealthiest landowners and slave owners in Maryland. The club boasted old and distinguished Maryland names such as Charles B. Calvert, John S. Skinner, Nicholas B. Worthington, Robert Bowie, John

H. Sothoron, Allen Bowie Davis and William N. Mercer. From near Baltimore came Ramsey McHenry, Charles Carroll, John Merryman and Thomas Swann, to name a few. Charles saw that Prince George's County's demographics were changing as it was losing farmers to big cities like Baltimore and the land was not producing as much as before. Due to the overuse of the land for the growing of tobacco, the soil began to lose its value, and diminished land value led to the southern Maryland "planter class" to push for a college to advance "scientific agriculture."

The Maryland Agricultural College, chartered on March 6, 1856, by the Maryland General Assembly, was one of the first institutions of agricultural

Charles Benedict Calvert, founder of the Maryland Agricultural College. *Library of Congress, Prints and Photographs Division.*

research in the country. Shortly after the school's formation, a special committee called the Maryland Agriculture Society was tasked with financing the proposed college. The committee suggested the sale of stock certificates that were valued at $50 each. On March 6, 1856, the Maryland General Assembly passed the Act to Endow an Agriculture College, and the college was chartered as a private college with the condition that the trustees raise $50,000 within two years. On January 5, 1858, the stockholders elected a board of trustees that included one representative from each Maryland county and one from the city of Baltimore (this arrangement was later amended to include trustees from the Western and Eastern Shores and the District of Columbia), and shares were sold at $25 each. Robert Bowie, of Prince George's County, was in charge of canvassing and collecting the funds. The Maryland Agricultural College was incorporated with the right to offer degrees and the agreement that the institution would be provided with a state appropriation of $6,000 a year. The stock split several times but never paid a dividend.

Despite the optimism of the planters and several large purchases by Charles Calvert, William Mercer and William Corcoran, the committee had raised only $43,000 by September 1, 1857. In 1858, the Maryland legislators tried to assist in raising additional funds by lowering the price of a share to $5, as the farming class and the General Assembly was reluctant to support a private institution. The primary investors were prominent businessmen in their own right and early trustees and financial backers in the new institution. As the smaller farmers and the state legislators were distrustful of the larger planters, they raised only another $500 at the new sale price. Charles Calvert and Benjamin Hallowell both shared the hope that with the new charter, the college would instill gentlemanly values and engage in scientific research and serve as a place where their poorer neighbors could learn to work harder and acquire a trade or profession.

The largest stockholder was William Mercer, a Maryland tobacco farmer who, following bankruptcy, moved to Louisiana to make a fortune in sugar. Charles Calvert owned more than 176 shares, while W.W. Corcoran, a Washington banker who founded the Corcoran Gallery of Art, bought forty shares and Johns Hopkins of Baltimore bought twenty. The shareholders elected a board of trustees to purchase land for the college, erect buildings and determine a course of study to include animal husbandry and scientific research.

In charge of finding a home for the Maryland Agricultural College was a search committee that considered several plots of land before deciding on the final location. Potential locations included land in Montgomery and Baltimore Counties, as well as in Laurel, Maryland, and each site was measured on its advantages and disadvantages. Benjamin Hallowell recommended that the college not be near a railroad station or a site that was too rural. In 1858, the final location for the college was selected in Prince George's County on 428 acres in the Bladensburg-Vansville district near Calvert's home, Riverdale Plantation. Mr. Hallowell felt that the final site was too isolated, but in the end, with its acreage totaling more than 400 acres, it was ideal. The land used for the college was purchased from Charles Calvert for $20,000. Calvert was so committed to the college that he offered the trustees attractive payment terms of $8,000 in cash and $3,400 in stock. In addition, he would remain the college's creditor for the remaining $10,000 at a 6 percent interest rate. However, records show that Calvert received only two payments of $600 each and that, after his death, his younger brother George Calvert unsuccessfully attempted to collect on the debt.

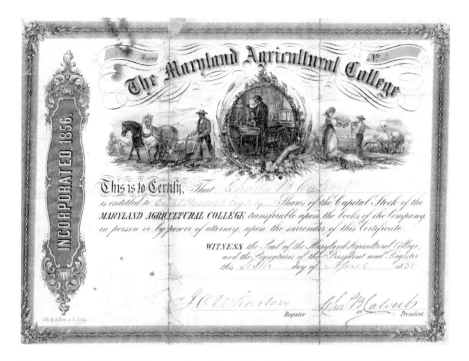

Maryland Agricultural College stock certificate signed by Charles B. Calvert. *Courtesy of University of Maryland Archives.*

On October 6, 1859, the college officially opened with thirty-four students, several domestic animals and farm laborers, three professors, one registrar and an absent president. The opening ceremonies were lavish. The keynote speaker was Joseph Henry, the celebrated scientist and founding secretary of the Smithsonian Institution. Additional attendees included Jacob Thompson, U.S. secretary of the interior; James Moore Wayne, an associate justice of the U.S. Supreme Court; Thomas Kirkpatrick, the inspector of agricultural schools in Ireland; William Pinkney, an Episcopal bishop of Washington, D.C.; William W. Corcoran, the Washington banker and philanthropist; and Charles Benedict Calvert, founder of the college and president of the board of trustees. The Barracks, located on the campus hilltop, was the first building constructed and contained eight lecture rooms, an auditorium, a kitchen and living quarters for up to 104 students. The Barracks also boasted the modern conveniences of the day, which included bathrooms and steam heating. The new campus consisted of four buildings and three barns. Thirteen of the thirty-four students were related to the founders, namely the Calvert, Carroll, Bowie, Paca, Goldsborough, Wharton,

Left: Unidentified MAC student in uniform. *Courtesy of University of Maryland Archives.*

Below: Maryland Agricultural College registration including the names of William and Robert Waring. *Courtesy of University of Maryland Archives.*

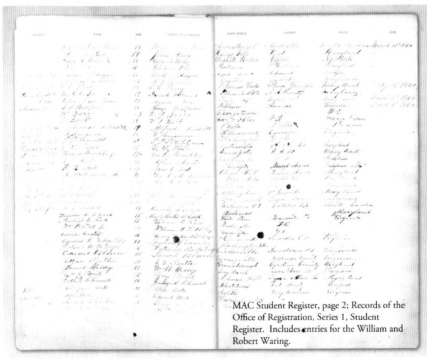

MAC Student Register, page 2; Records of the Office of Registration, Series 1, Student Register. Includes entries for the William and Robert Waring.

Sothoron, Sands and Skinners families. The remaining students were scions of well-established families from all over the state. MAC was one of the most expensive colleges in the country, at $260 a year, effectively removing it from the economic range of most farmers' sons. Each of the new students wore a uniform and followed a very strict schedule that included classes on moral and intellectual culture and instruction, as well as working together in the agricultural fields and military drills.

While western Maryland was pro-Union, Prince George's County and other southern counties were home to many slaveholders and thus were sympathetic and anxious to support the new Confederacy. When the Confederate army fired the first shot at the Union soldiers at Fort Sumter, South Carolina, in 1859, the future for the college changed dramatically. In the fall of 1860, MAC began with seventy-eight students on its registration rolls, but by July 1861, it had only seventeen students, an example of the initial impact the Civil War had on the college. Many of the students came from families who were large slaveholders and whose economy depended on tobacco and cotton plantations driven by slave labor. By the time the war was underway, Prince George's County's concern about the status of slavery and states' rights was getting visibly stronger. The college had already started to lose financial support as many of its Southern students and faculty headed south to enlist in the Maryland Unit for the Confederate army in Richmond, while others enlisted in the Union army. During the first years of the war, the new mathematics department chair, Professor Joseph Hart Chenoworth, resigned from the college and joined the Thirty-first Virginia; he was killed at the Battle of Port Republic on June 9, 1862. Although it was readily apparent to the administration that a large number of students and faculty were Southern sympathizers, the college managed to keep its doors open despite the ongoing war. But finances were extremely tight during the war.

In 1862, the college awarded its first degrees to William B. Sands and Thomas Franklin under President Onderdonk. Also in 1862, President Abraham Lincoln signed the Morrill Land Grant Act, which provided federal funds to schools that taught agriculture and engineering or provided military training. In February 1864, the Maryland Agricultural College officially became a land-grant institution. Ironically, the Morrill Act and the contemporaneous Homestead Act, which offered cheap western land to homesteaders, became law only after the departure of Southern legislators from the U.S. Congress in 1861. The acts had been proposed prior to the war, but Southern congressmen had blocked these acts because they considered the legislation a threat to the expansion of slavery in the territories.

The Barracks was the first building constructed on the campus of the Maryland Agricultural College. *Library of Congress, Prints and Photographs Division.*

The Maryland Agricultural College Board of Trustees consisted of men from all over the state who were wealthy farmers and dabbled in politics. The board represented many from the Eastern Shore, the western counties and southern Maryland who were prominent planters, early trustees and large stockholders in the new institution. Each county and the city of Baltimore were represented on the board; however, because sixteen of the twenty-four members were slave owners pushing for the state's secession, the college nearly died in its infancy. Trustee John Merryman, a stockholder and farmer from Baltimore County and a lieutenant in a state militia called the Baltimore County Horse Guards, was the subject of the most famous legal challenge to Abraham Lincoln's suspension of the writ of habeas corpus. Merryman, a vocal Southern supporter, advocated that the state of Maryland secede from the Union. On May 25, 1861, Merryman was arrested for treason and imprisoned at Fort McHenry by Federal troops. Merryman was later released on bail; the case never went to trial, and the charges were finally dropped in 1867. The most prominent of the board was Charles Benedict Calvert of Prince George's County, who served as the first president of the board.

EARLY LEADERSHIP

The selection of the college's president and faculty was one of the most important decisions the trustees had to make in order to prepare the college for success. The man chosen as president needed to be committed to more than just teaching the young men how to effectively manage their land. He needed to be willing to use scientific research to yield the best produce and livestock that the farm could produce. Finding a qualified man to lead the young masters of the future was crucial to the survival of the college as well as the community.

In 1859, Benjamin Hallowell was selected as the first president of the Maryland Agricultural College. Hallowell was a well-known and respected educator, scientist and farmer from Montgomery County who had advised the trustees on organizing the college, faculty and buildings. Hallowell's position on agriculture reform made him an ideal candidate as president of the new institution. In addition to being known for his ideas on agricultural reform, Mr. Hallowell was a retired Quaker abolitionist whose hometown of Sandy Spring, Maryland, was a station on the Underground Railroad. Hallowell's farms were a showcase for free labor, a prime example on how to operate a farm without the use of slavery. He accepted the position as president on the condition that the college did not use slaves, and he would not accept a salary. During the planning, Hallowell developed a core curriculum designed to maximize the skills and knowledge of all the professors charged to create a unique university of agricultural research. After one month on the job, Hallowell abruptly resigned, citing ill health as the reason. There had been speculation that it was not ill health that caused Hallowell to resign but rather the issue of slavery that existed among the president, the board of trustees and many of the students.

Charles Benedict Calvert assumed the position of acting president following the resignation of Benjamin Hallowell, and he served in this capacity from 1859 until 1861. Enrollment under Calvert's tenure almost doubled from thirty-five to sixty-three students. He established a non-credit preparatory program for applicants who could not meet the college's academic requirements. Calvert also hired Professor Townsend Glover to teach the students botany and entomology

In 1860, Reverend John Work Scott was elected by the board of trustees to assume the presidency. At the time of his election on April 13, 1860, Scott was serving as president of Washington College in Pennsylvania, known today as Washington and Jefferson College. He voluntarily retired from the presidency of Washington College prior to its merger with Jefferson College and completed his career in higher education teaching at West Virginia University. He retired from teaching and never assumed the role as MAC's president.

John Colby was the principal of the Allegany County Academy in Cumberland, Maryland, when he was elected president of MAC in July 1860. The college's enrollment peaked at fifty-eight during his tenure but dropped off sharply with the approach of war. Colby resigned during the 1860–61 academic year.

From 1861 to 1864, Henry Onderdonk was president of the college. Prior to his selection, Onderdonk was a Quaker educator working in Baltimore. Under his three-year tenure, eight students received degrees. Onderdonk resigned under accusations (never substantiated) that he willingly harbored and entertained Confederate troops under the command of General Bradley T. Johnson, who had encamped on the college grounds.

By the time Henry Onderdonk had taken office, the effects of the war were already starting to show a financial strain on the college, as attendance was low. In 1861, during his tenure, rumors of Confederate cavalrymen visiting the college on numerous occasions, as well as the infamous "Old South Ball," were reportedly held on campus at the Rossborough Inn, a private residence at the time. It was said that Confederate general Bradley used the Rossborough Inn as his headquarters and entertained his officers and the daughters of Prince George's County's wealthiest planters until early hours in the morning at the ball. President Onderdonk vehemently denied that he was present at any of the alleged visits and stated that no such ball was ever held on campus. However, the Unionists in the Maryland General Assembly were not pleased with the "rumors" and threatened to withhold financial support, forcing Onderdonk to resign in 1864. After resigning, Onderdonk opened a private academy in Baltimore and concluded his education career as headmaster of St. James School in Hagerstown, Maryland, a position he held until the time of his death in 1895.

The Maryland Agricultural College aspired to be the first institution where agricultural research was the primary focus. In that vein, the trustees made every effort to recruit the best minds of the most learned and scientific gentlemen in the great state of Maryland. Benjamin Hallowell, who would eventually assume the role as first president, was also appointed to be a professor of moral and mental philosophy, history and English literature. Other illustrious MAC faculty members included George C. Schaeffer, AM, MD, who was a professor of the science of agriculture, including chemistry and its application to the arts, geology and mineralogy; H.D. Gough, AB, a professor of exact sciences, including mathematics (pure and mixed), surveying, menstruation, engineering and construction, mechanics and astronomy; and Battista Lorino, LLD, a professor of ancient and modern languages, including Latin, Greek, French, German, Spanish and Italian. The aforementioned men were experts in their respective fields and were perfect for the planned education and research program designed for the college. The positions of physiology, comparative anatomy and veterinary surgery, as well as botany, entomology and ornithology, were to be filled later.

THE WAR'S IMPACT ON THE COLLEGE

Located on the border between Washington, D.C., and the North and the Confederate state of Virginia, the state of Maryland had to be forcibly held in the Union. Following the Baltimore Riots of 1861, President Lincoln immediately filed a habeas corpus and threatened anyone who spoke of joining the Confederacy or openly advocated the secession of Maryland from the Union. The war had placed a serious hardship on the college because of its geographic location and proximity to Washington. The college was also strategically located close to the Baltimore & Ohio (B&O) Railroad route, making it necessary for Union soldiers to guard the border between the Federal city and Maryland against the Confederate army. Strategically located on Washington Turnpike (now U.S. Route 1), the college was often used by Confederate officers as a resting place to gather their troops before going to Silver Spring in Montgomery County.

The Federal government did consider commandeering the college for a five-hundred-bed military hospital, but this never came to pass. It goes without saying that extraordinary measures by the Federal government were taken to suppress the activity of students and faculty at the college. For example, an editorial in the *Washington National Republican* in September 1861 complained of drunken soldiers in the nearby Bladensburg-Vansville district and the need for the provost marshal to enforce the prohibition of alcohol sales to soldiers. Despite the turmoil engulfing Maryland and the nation and the fact that many of the students and faculty of the agricultural college were Southern sympathizers, the college continued to operate during the war and was able to graduate its first class in July 1862.

ROSSBOROUGH INN

In 1822, George Calvert purchased the plot of what was once known as the Rossborough Farm from John Ross. In 1837, he deeded this land to his sons Charles and George Calvert. Charles Benedict included this plot and the house in the 428 acres that would eventually become the Maryland Agricultural College. Prior to the war, Rossborough was a private residence, and during the war, the inn was used as a temporary camp by the Confederate army. In April 1864, Union general Ambrose E. Burnside, moving from Annapolis to Washington, camped his six thousand troops on the college grounds. The troops destroyed some fences, and the college sued the government in vain for damages. Three months later, Confederate general Bradley T. Johnson, a Marylander, swept through with at least four hundred men, threatening Washington from the rear. On July 11, Johnson set up headquarters at the Rossborough Inn, and his men camped around it. Students and officials at the college welcomed them warmly. Legend has it that the college officials provided food for the soldiers, and young women appeared from the surrounding neighborhood. Fifes and fiddles came out, and partying lasted into the night.

The Rossborough Inn, purchased by George Calvert and sold to MAC by son Charles B. Calvert, is the oldest building on the college's campus. *Library of Congress, Prints and Photographs Division.*

Photo of Professor Joseph Chenoworth and his sister Mary. Chenoworth resigned from MAC to join the CSA. *Virginia Military Institute Archives.*

THE WAR CAUSES THE COLLEGE TO LOSE STUDENTS AND FACULTY

The Civil War had a great impact on MAC, as the college was in its infancy stage when war was declared. In the spring and summer of 1861, the first MAC students with deep Confederate ties to Virginia and North Carolina left the college. When President Lincoln filed his habeas corpus to prevent Maryland from seceding from the Union, there was a mass exodus of students leaving the college to enlist in either the Confederate or Union armies. The first documented enlistment was that of Private Josiah Crudup of Granville County, North Carolina, on April 22, 1861. Private Crudup was a member of the Twelfth North Carolina Infantry, the Granville Greys, and died of disease within four months. Other MAC students who enlisted included Junius B. Hodges of Nansemond County, who enlisted on June 5, 1861, and died of pneumonia on October 27, 1864; Robert B. Waring and his younger brother William W. Waring of Upper Marlboro, Maryland; Raleigh W. Kirk of Lancaster County, Virginia; and Private John Hill and Captain William H. Henderson of the Virginia Infantry. In 1862, the twenty-six-year-old son of MAC college professor Dr. John Wharton was arrested as a Confederate spy and detained in Washington's infamous Old Capitol Prison, where he was subsequently shot and killed by a guard for sticking his head out the window.

Located in an agricultural district in southern Maryland dominated by planters dependent on slave labor, MAC was founded as an institution that conceded the efficacy—and perhaps the advantage—of free labor. However, the commitment to training students in the management of farms without using slave labor can be seen in Hallowell's acceptance of the presidency. This dual founding in both slavery and freedom illustrates the conflicted origins of the Maryland Agricultural College and its founders. The changes that motivated the creation of the college drew together Calvert and Hallowell, both of whom believed in the agricultural reform necessary to address the economical issues affecting the state's future in farming.

In 1866, continued losses in financial resources and the strain of the war caused the college to briefly close its doors. In 1867, the college was reopened as a state school and renamed the University of Maryland. Despite the fact that no slave labor contributed to the building of the Maryland Agricultural College/University of Maryland, the legacy of slavery and Jim Crow meant that the college would remain a segregated institution until the 1950s. A separate but equal institution was established on the Eastern Shore, where the Princess Anne Academy became a part of the University of Maryland for colored students.

The founders of the Maryland Agricultural College envisioned an institution that would supersede their original goals and look to the future of farming in the state of Maryland. The college transformed the students into cultured gentlemen, knowledgeable about the classics and able to read Greek and Latin and to discuss the great events of the day. More important, however, is that they learned how to improve the quality of the farms through crop rotation, take better care of their livestock through animal husbandry and understand agricultural research. Many of the former students who survived the war would make great contributions to society in politics, business and education.

Chapter 3

Protecting the Federal City

In the early days of the war, Washington, D.C., was a city with little military defense. Not only was the District short on troops, but it was also short on defensive posts. The city had only between four hundred and five hundred troops—mainly U.S. Marines and ordnance men—and just four small local volunteer organizations: two companies of riflemen, one battalion of infantry and one other battalion.[5] As the Southern states seceded from the Union in the months leading up to the war, government leaders worried about the city's defenses. In order to protect the nation's capital, the government needed to keep the transportation and communication lines open in the District and northern Prince George's County. The government established a navy unit called the Potomac Flotilla to secure Union communications in the Chesapeake Bay and the Potomac River as well as to disrupt Confederate communications and shipping. The unit patrolled Prince George's County's shorelines and inlets.[6]

The government assigned Colonel Charles P. Stone with the job of raising more troops. By spring, Stone had organized thirty-three companies of infantry and riflemen and two troops of cavalry, which included D.C. volunteers.[7] It was not until the start of the war—the firing on Fort Sumter in April 1861—that the government decided to take serious action. Government leaders rushed in Federal and state troops to defend the District, initially giving them the task of building forts and batteries to aid in that defense.[8] Rather than going off to fight, many of the troops called up in the last months of the war stayed in and around D.C. and Maryland to protect the capital. Troops were scattered along the Baltimore & Ohio rail line to Baltimore, in camps throughout the District, in Bladensburg and in the string of hastily built forts surrounding the city.[9]

No battles were actually fought in Prince George's County, but Union forces were always present, guarding the railroad line, marching through the countryside and watching from the forts.[10] By the end of the war, the government had built sixty-eight permanent and temporary military structures around the District that were designed to resist attacks from ground forces such as infantry, cavalry and artillery.[11] These forts were supported by ninety-three detached batteries for field guns, twenty miles of rifle pits and covered ways, wooden blockhouses at three key points, thirty-two miles of military road, several stockade bridgeheads and four advance picket stations. Emplacements for 1,501 field and siege guns, of which 807 guns and 98 mortars were in place, were set up along the thirty-seven-mile circle of forts. Prince George's County was home to three of the structures that protected the District: Fort Washington, Fort Foote and Fort Lincoln.

FORT WASHINGTON

Other than a few guns at the Washington Arsenal, Fort Washington was the District of Columbia's only defense at the beginning of the Civil War. Fort Washington, located on the east bank of the Potomac River, stands on Digges Point—land that was originally part of Warburton Manor, the colonial estate of Thomas A. Digges. The government built Fort Washington in 1824 to replace an earlier structure, Fort Warburton. Built in 1809, Fort Warburton was destroyed during the War of 1812 by its own garrison in 1814 to prevent its capture by the British. Major Pierre L'Enfant was sent to design a new defensive structure twelve days later, but he was soon replaced by Lieutenant Colonel Walker K. Armistead. Completed on October 2, 1824, Fort Washington was built to protect the Potomac River approach for the city and its defenders from the enemy.[12] Fort Washington had parapets and casemates—fortified gun emplacements or armored structures where the guns were fired from—to provide mountings for the artillery and to protect the garrison. The buildings housed the garrison and provided space for a variety of military activities. The casemates were vaulted brick rooms with openings in the outer wall through which the cannons could fire.

Aerial view of Fort Washington, which was the only fort protecting Washington, D.C., at the beginning of the war. *Library of Congress, Prints and Photographs Division.*

The fort was designed to have cannons mounted in twenty-six casemate openings, but only six were mounted. The weaponry was the most important part of the fort's existence and purpose. The guns in the fort's water battery were 53 feet above the water level, the casemate guns were 89 feet above the river and the guns mounted to fire over the wall were 115 feet above the water. The fort's twenty-four- and thirty-two-pounders had a range of more than one mile from the river and would subject an enemy ship coming up the Potomac River to heavy fire.[13] Soldiers from the First, Third and Fourth U.S. Artillery occupied the fort's masonry during its early history.[14] However, Fort Washington had fallen into disuse by 1840. Congress allocated money to repair and expand the structure. The fort was extensively remodeled in the 1840s, and its first guns were mounted in 1846.[15] The government withdrew the garrison in 1853, dismounting all guns and abandoning the fort. The enlisted men's barracks remained empty until war broke out between the Northern and Southern states.

Secretary of the Navy Gideon Welles issued the first order for the defense of Washington, D.C., on January 5, 1861, assigning forty marines to protect

Fort Washington's main gate. *Library of Congress, Prints and Photographs Division.*

Fort Washington's drawbridge gate. *Library of Congress, Prints and Photographs Division.*

Fort Washington. The Union garrisoned the fort as the outer defense for the District to protect it from Confederate forces in Maryland and Virginia. Artillery had to be remounted at the start of the Civil War because no heavy artillery had been mounted at the fort between October 1853 and 1860. In the first two years of the war, the amount of ordnance at the fort more than doubled. In 1862, the fort reached its peak wartime complement of eighty pieces, which remained in place without additions until after the war.[16]

Companies of the First and Fourth Artilleries and state artillery units passed through Fort Washington during the war, which brought more troops to Fort Washington than its quarters could house.[17] The fort was designed to house only 60, but in 1861, it had 280 enlisted men with Company D, First United States Artillery; the Company of Recruits; the Logan Guards; and the Washington Artillerists. Housing remained a problem throughout the war. In June 1862, 117 enlisted men were on post; 272 enlisted men were there in March 1863; 146 enlisted men were on post in May 1864; and 142 enlisted men were there in July 1865.[18] The troops had to use other buildings and tents to relieve overcrowding as every possible space in the fort was used, from the brick enlisted men's barracks to the attic.

Considered an unhealthy post, the fort had a need for an adequate medical facility since it was first built. Half of the enlisted men's barracks was used as a hospital when the fort was first garrisoned. A separate facility was needed because of the large number of men at the post during the Civil War. A hospital with two wards for sixteen patients was built outside the fort's walls in 1863 after post commander Colonel Henry Merchant requested a facility to house twenty-five to one hundred men the previous year.[19] The Invalid Corps of the Fourth United States Artillery was quartered at the fort in December 1863. Post life expanded beyond the defensive walls of the fort and raveling during the last years of the war. In addition to the hospital, a complex of other buildings was erected to the north and northeast of the commanding officers' quarters, including a new barracks for enlisted men, three double houses for officers' quarters, a chapel (which also served as a schoolhouse), laundresses' quarters and a post bakery.

Although they had junior officers to assist them, post commanders had the overall direction of the post. The commander was responsible for the overall condition of the fort, including the building and ordnance, and for his troops' well-being. The adjutants carried out much of the commanding officers' clerical work and acted as executive secretaries. They were responsible for activities, including parades; reviews; inspections; and work, picket and guard details.

One of the cannons at Fort Washington. *Library of Congress, Prints and Photographs Division.*

The Battle of Hampton Roads on March 9, 1862, between the USS *Monitor*—the first ironclad warship commissioned by the U.S. Navy during the war—and the Confederate ironclad CSS *Virginia*, highlighted Fort Washington's vulnerability and created panic in the nation's capital. This battle was the first fought between two armored warships and ended in a standoff in which neither side could claim victory. Even though the *Virginia* never attacked Union ships again, the government was concerned that another ironclad ship might slip past the isolated guns of Fort Washington and begin a bombardment of the city.[20]

In addition, many European countries seemed eager to join the fight on the side of the Confederacy as the war progressed. The government was concerned such intervention would add a major naval threat to the city. Secretary of War Edwin Stanton appointed a commission to examine the city's defenses.[21] The commission came to the conclusion that even though the city had sufficient defensive works, including Fort

John G. Barnard, chief military engineer in charge of
fortifying Washington, D.C., during the Civil War. *Library of
Congress, Prints and Photographs Division.*

Washington, to protect the city from land attack, the District was still
vulnerable to attack from water. According to the commission's report:

> *The commission furthers their opinion that the Defense of Washington
> cannot be considered complete without the defense of the river against an
> enemy's armed vessels. Foreign intervention would bring against us always
> in superior naval force on the Potomac, and we are, even now, threatened
> with Confederate iron-clads fitted in English Ports.* [22]

As it was sixteen miles below the city, Fort Washington was too far away to be adequately supported. Colonel John Gross Barnard, the chief military engineer for the city's defenses, and other army engineers went to work on the commission's recommendation. They began building earthworks to resist naval bombardment, which decreased Fort Washington's military importance.[23]

FORT FOOTE

The commission's report pointed out an area near Roziers Bluff, a one-hundred-foot-high cliff six miles south of Washington, D.C., on the Potomac River, as an excellent site for a new fort. Surrounded by a large swamp, the commanding bluff was on the Maryland shore just north of Fort Washington.[24] The report suggested constructing a battery of ten guns and a covering work, stating also that a fort on the site would be easily communicated with by water.[25] The layout would largely follow the plans laid out in West Point instructor Dennis Mahan's "A Treatise on Field Fortification," which noted:

> *As a field fort must rely entirely on its own strength, it should be constructed with such care that the enemy will be forced to abandon an attempt to storm it, and be obliged to resort to the method of regular approaches used in the attack of permanent works. To affect this, all the ground around the fort, within range of the cannon, should offer no shelter to the enemy from its fire; the ditches should be flanked throughout; and the relief is so great as to preclude any attempt at scaling the work.*[26]

Construction on the new fort began in the winter of 1862–63 but progressed slowly due to the initial difficulty of obtaining labor. However, this problem was resolved when the fort was first garrisoned on August 12, 1863, by four companies of the Ninth New York Heavy Artillery Regiment.[27] The soldiers were immediately pressed into service as laborers on the project. The fort was completed and certified ready for action in the fall of 1863.[28] The structure was named Fort Foote in honor of Rear Admiral Andrew H. Foote, who commanded the Mississippi River Squadron from 1861 to 1862 and died of wounds on June 26, 1863. Fort Foote was one of the largest military structures near the nation's capital during the Civil War, as well as a main unit in the system of military structures surrounding the city. Fort Foote was designed to defend the city against an attack from Confederate ships coming up the river.[29]

Fort Foote and Battery Rogers, located across the Potomac in Alexandria, Virginia, were the only seacoast forts near the District. Fort Foote was built as a water battery of eight two-hundred-pounder Parrott rifles and two fifteen-inch guns that cost $9,000 each. However, due to delays in casting and the demands of guns needed for combat in Virginia, the fort was not fully armed right from the start. The first fifteen-inch Rodman gun arrived in late 1863, and others arrived at various points over the next two years. The fort was not completely armed until April 1865, just before the final surrender of Confederate forces in Virginia, and was not

Commander Andrew Hull Foote, after whom Fort Foote was named, in military uniform. *Library of Congress, Prints and Photographs Division.*

pronounced complete until June 6, 1865.[30] The guns could do major damage to a wooden warship, and ironclad ships could not even stand at close range against the massive weapons, which were much larger than any guns defending Washington from the land.

The garrison at Fort Foote was housed in wood-frame buildings outside the confines of the fort rather than inside the fort, like most seacoast fortifications. The use of iron in the fortifications was limited due to the fort's location along the coast. Most of the fort was constructed of earth and locally cut lumber. The revetments and the vertical walls of the interior structure were made almost wholly of cedar posts, while the roofing of the structures was made of chestnut logs, according to an 1881 report on the defenses by General Barnard.[31] The fort had strong earthen embankments to withstand potential attacks from the new rifled ordnance. The military took care to ensure that the fort could resist moisture and naval shells. The front of the fort was over five hundred feet long, and the earth walls were twenty feet thick.[32]

The daily routine at Fort Foote was similar to that at other forts in the region.[33] However, duty at Fort Foote was considered unpleasant and hazardous. Mosquitoes plagued the post with malaria during the summer, while typhoid was a constant threat due to the lack of easily obtained pure water. The area was so malarial that neighboring inhabitants had long referred to it as "the graveyard of Prince George's County."[34] The ten- by forty-foot hospital was completely filled at any given time during the summer with as much as half the garrison on the sick list. Fort Foote's troops were some distance from the nightlife in Washington and Alexandria and were rarely granted furlough.[35]

The troops at Fort Foote normally began their day with reveille before sunrise immediately followed by morning muster, at which they were counted and reported for sick call. After muster, soldiers performed drill details, including gunnery practice and parade drills. They also did work such as improving the fort's defenses, broken by meal and rest breaks, until taps at 8:30 or 9:00 p.m. On Sundays, following muster, the troops had morning inspections and church call followed by leisure time in the afternoon, which was usually filled by writing letters home, bathing or simply catching up on sleep.

Fort Foote was considered an isolated post, as the nearest land route, Piscataway Road, was over a mile away. The road was used only if the Potomac River froze over and water traffic was impossible. The fort conducted nearly all communication by the river wharf at the bottom of the bluff. A mail boat stopped at the fort three times a week. Daily boats to Alexandria and Washington were only for officers, visitors and other officials.[36] Alfred Seelye Roe, a soldier in Company A of the New York Ninth Heavy Artillery, detailed his experience at Fort Foote in his self-published book, *The Ninth New York Heavy Artillery*. He described several instances of soldiers amusing themselves with tricks and pranks. On one instance, one particular soldier known for his love of whiskey smuggled a quantity of liquor out of Alexandria by hiding his flasks in a child's coffin. He crossed the river pretending to be a grieving father and made it back into camp.[37]

Lieutenant Colonel William H. Seward Jr., son of U.S. secretary of state William Seward, commanded the post. On August 20, 1863, Seward, President Abraham Lincoln, Secretary of War Edwin Stanton and the recently promoted General Barnard visited the new construction. Secretary

Seward and his wife visited the post often while their son was in command. They regularly went to the fort with parties of distinguished visitors to watch the troops' demonstrations. The Sewards attended a training drill on one scheduled occasion during which the fort's gunners planned on using a target anchored two miles away in the middle of the Potomac. Having learned of the scheduled target practice, Confederate sympathizers rowed out from the Virginia shore, cut the target loose and towed it away. The embarrassed Union gunners had to fire on other targets while Mrs. Seward conducted an impromptu lunch in one of the fort's bunkers.[38]

Every regularly scheduled gunnery was attended by Washington residents, mainly prominent citizens, because of the fort's relative proximity to the city and the enormous size of its guns. A large crowd of Washingtonians attended the inaugural firing of the fort's fifteen-inch guns on February 27, 1864. The enormous smoothbore cannons weighed 25 tons and required 45 pounds of powder to send a 440-pound round shot over five thousand yards. The guns were fired once more on April 1, 1864.[39]

The Sewards visited the fort on October 22, 1864, with U.S. secretary of the treasury Salmon P. Chase, U.S. secretary of the navy Gideon Welles and General Barnard to commemorate the first firing of the fort's new two-hundred-pounder Parrott rifles. But at that point, the Civil War was beginning to wind down, and Washingtonians questioned the postwar usefulness of the city's line of forts. Secretary Welles said, "It is a strong position, and a vast amount of labor has been expended—uselessly expended. In going over the works a melancholy feeling came over me, that there should have been so much waste, for the fort is not wanted, and will never fire a hostile gun. No hostile fleet will ever ascend the Potomac."[40]

FORT LINCOLN

Major General George B. McClellan, who assumed supreme command of the Union army on July 27, 1861, began an accelerated program of reorganization and rebuilding. McClellan ordered then-colonel Barnard to begin immediate clearing of woodland to the south of the city and construction of fortification. An area in Bladensburg, along the Maryland-D.C. border, became a staging area for numerous newly organized and already-established Union contingents. The site, where the Battle of Bladensburg took place in 1814, once again saw military activity.

One camp, which included the northernmost portion of the area, was designated Camp Union. The First and Eleventh Massachusetts, the Second New Hampshire and the Twenty-sixth Pennsylvania Regiments, all of which were formed into a brigade under the command of General Joseph Hooker, stayed in the camp. They pitched their tents "upon the old battlefield, and the old dueling grounds were within their lines and proved admirably adapted for target practice," according to regimental records.[41]

President Lincoln, with Secretary Seward and U.S. Navy secretary Gideon Welles, journeyed to Bladensburg to review the troops on August 25, 1861. The following day, General Hooker's brigade broke ground on a new fortification in the same location. The fort, named in honor of President Lincoln in September 1861, was situated at a strategic point overlooking the extensive valley formed by the Eastern Branch and its tributaries and commanding the Baltimore Turnpike, the Baltimore & Ohio Railroad and several minor roads, which, passing through or near Bladensburg, led into the District.[42] Hooker's brigade was the first to occupy the fort, while Captain T.S. Paddock was in immediate command.

General Joseph Hooker. *Library of Congress, Prints and Photographs Division.*

On February 27, 1862, the Second Pennsylvania Veteran Heavy Artillery took over duty at Fort Lincoln, which was established as the regimental headquarters. Colonel A.A. Gibson arrived at the fort and assumed command of the regiment on August 3, 1862. The Second Pennsylvania Veteran Heavy Artillery strengthened fortifications at Fort Lincoln. The troops also constructed a line of rifle pits near the old Spring House, which was built long before the fort. They also built Battery Jameson, a powerful concentration

An interior view of Fort Lincoln in 1865. *Library of Congress, Prints and Photographs Division.*

Gun crews of Company H, Third Massachusetts Heavy Artillery, standing at the ready at Fort Lincoln. *Library of Congress, Prints and Photographs Division.*

of artillery reinforcing the fort. The battery, named after Brigadier General Charles D. Jameson, who was in the Battle of Bull Run, was connected to the fort in a covered way. Four twelve-pounder field cannons and one twenty-four-pound barbette—an armored enclosure used to protect cannon—was in place at Battery James, according to an 1864 report.[43]

Colonel Gibson organized a band of musicians from the enlisted ranks. Under the direction of a Professor Perrie, this band soon gained great favor with President Lincoln and performed at the White House almost daily. According to informal reports, President Lincoln made several visits to Fort Lincoln and Battery Jameson, including during a grand review of batteries on December 15, 1863.[44] On many of his trips to the acreage, the president sat on a peaceful knoll shaded by a giant oak tree, where he read, napped, reviewed the troops and drank at the spring beneath the tree.[45] He considered it a respite from the pressures of his regular working day.

The fort was also home to Company E, Fourth U.S. Colored Infantry, organized in July 1863 and made mostly of former slaves from Maryland as

Company E, Fourth U.S. Colored Infantry, at Fort Lincoln in 1864. *Library of Congress, Prints and Photographs Division.*

Photo of unidentified U.S. Colored Troops soldier. *Library of Congress, Prints and Photographs Division.*

well as those from North Carolina who fought in Petersburg and Richmond, Virginia. The infantry was one of 166 African American regiments in the Union army. Planters in Prince George's County complained that Union soldiers encouraged their slaves to leave their plantations and enlist in the Union army. Many slaves from the county did indeed slip across the D.C. line and gain freedom by serving as soldiers for the Union.[46]

LAUREL FACTORY

The Southern states did not frequently test the Union's troops stationed at the forts in Prince George's County or the protection they provided to D.C. Confederate general Jubal Early's final invasion of Maryland in July 1864 was one exception. Early brought a large Confederate force in from the west, causing havoc in Prince George's County and panic in the District.[47] Brigadier General Bradley T. Johnson, a Marylander who reported to General Early on General Robert E. Lee's orders, was asked to move four hundred cavalrymen north of Baltimore and then between Baltimore and Washington, D.C., on July 11. The troops blew up railroad lines and cut telegraph lines along the way.[48] Johnson was then ordered to swing around the city, cutting the Baltimore & Ohio Washington Branch near Laurel, finally pushing toward the U.S. government prison Point Lookout with intentions to release Confederate prisoners. Johnson encountered a large Union presence in Laurel—a significant manufacturing center with Northern ties—and had to move south to Beltsville.[49] Johnson and his men eventually rejoined Early's forces for an unsuccessful attack on Fort Stevens in the District.[50]

Laurel, known at the time as "Laurel Factory," was home to several Union units, including the 141st New York and the Ninth Corps of the 109th New York Volunteer Regiment, guarding the Baltimore & Ohio rail line beginning in 1862. In April 1863, one soldier noted that they were the only regiment between Baltimore and Washington and that the engineers would not run a train if the guards were taken off.[51]

Sarah Palmer, a hospital matron who traveled with the 109th, wrote

Confederate general Jubal Early, who created havoc in Prince George's County when he moved through the area in an attempt to reach Washington, D.C. *Library of Congress, Prints and Photographs Division.*

Brigadier General Bradley T. Johnson, who commanded troops for General Early under orders from General Robert E. Lee. *William Emerson Strong Photograph Album, David M. Rubenstein Rare Book and Manuscript Library, Duke University.*

an account of her experiences in "Aunt Becky's Army Life." She was first at a hospital in Beltsville for four months before it moved to Laurel in January 1863. She described that hospital as an "old store and a two story dwelling house," a building that still stands at the intersection of Main and Avondale Streets. She wrote about supplies sent from the abolitionists in Sandy Spring, the pigs that the "boys" captured and hid in the basement, the panic caused by a rumor that General Lee's army was near and always about her compassion for the sick, wounded and dying.[52]

THE FORTS AFTER THE WAR

After the Civil War, Fort Washington was the only permanent defense unit for the District of Columbia until it was abandoned in 1872. From 1896 to 1921, the fort served as the headquarters for the Defense of the Potomac. In 1921, after the fort was no longer needed as a coast defense, it became the headquarters of the 12th Infantry. The fort headquartered many other army units over the years, including the 4th Artillery, 3rd Cavalry Band and 104th Co. Coast artillery. During World War II, the grounds were used for training army personnel, and barracks housed German prisoners of war.

Ownership of the site transferred from the War Department to the Department of the Interior in 1939. Shortly after Pearl Harbor, it reverted to the War Department; later, it was transferred to the Veterans' Administration. Finally, in 1946, the fort was returned to the Department of the Interior for park purposes. Rehabilitation of the old fort was begun in 1957 under the Mission 66 program. In the following years, the fort was open at various times for visitors and reenactments. The buildings deteriorated before being restored in 2000 by the National Park Service. Today, the site is a 340-acre visitor park with the barracks and fort restored, an 1857 lighthouse, several miles of hiking and bike trails, Civil War artillery, living history weekends and audio-visual history exhibits.[53]

Fort Foote never fired a shot against an opponent after Robert E. Lee's surrender on April 9, 1865. After the war, the government dismantled the District's defenses and returned most of the forts and property to their previous owners. Fort Foote, however, was one of the structures the government chose to retain. After some new construction, the government used the fort as a Federal military prison between 1868 and 1869.[54] The fort was also used as a testing ground for a recoil gun carriage. This did not last long, as commercial traffic resumed in the Potomac, making it unsafe to fire cannonballs over the river.[55] The government purchased the land from its owner in 1873 with plans to strengthen the fort. Construction began on improvements, but it was halted when the appropriation was withdrawn abruptly. Continued postwar military cutbacks caused the garrison to be removed in 1878 and the fort abandoned. Between 1902 and 1917, the fort was used as a training area for a local engineering school. Fort Foote was used during World War I for gas service training and during World War II for officer candidates from Fort Washington. The fort was transferred to the Department of the Interior and the National Park Service after World War II for inclusion in the service's system of national parks. The area is mostly forested today, though some of the original bastions have been preserved. Two fifteen-inch guns sit on carriages overlooking the Potomac, one originally used at Fort Foote and the other from Battery Rodgers.[56]

Fort Lincoln is now part of Fort Lincoln Cemetery and is open to the public. All of the fort's original buildings are gone except the old Spring House. Many of the larger trees within the cemetery may have been there during the war. The fort still has the colors standing proud, with three tarnished artillery guns protecting it. The battery looks out over the scenic grounds of the cemetery and beyond.

Chapter 4

Government

Maryland in the years preceding the Civil War had one foot in the South and the other in the North. If government is a true representation of the people that it serves, then each foot was well represented in the Maryland legislature. The issue of slavery was hotly debated in the Maryland General Assembly, whereas states' rights did not become an issue until the Civil War, as parts of the state of Maryland were occupied by Federal troops. From the first introduction of slaves to Maryland to the final days of the Civil War, the state's political parties, as well as the state legislature's position on slavery, evolved to reflect the changing role of slavery. The Maryland General Assembly, created in 1637, serves as the legislative body for the state. Similar to many state governments in the United States, the General Assembly is a bicameral legislature composed of two houses. The Maryland State Senate is the upper body of the house, and the lower body is the House of Delegates. Before, during and after the war, this chamber was the scene of many intense discussions regarding the issue of slavery as the state passed several laws that restricted the growth of slavery as well limited the freedom of the slave and debated the emancipation of Maryland slaves.

Presidential Election of 1860

The dueling interests of slavery and states' rights played a prominent role in national politics in the years preceding the Civil War. The Missouri Compromise of 1850, the Fugitive Slave Acts, the Kansas-Nebraska Act, the Supreme Court decision in *Dred Scott v. The State of Missouri* and the publication of *Uncle Tom's Cabin* were issues that played on the mindset of an already fragile and volatile electorate, many of whom were making their way to the polls to decide on who would succeed James Buchanan as president of the United States. The questions confronting the electorate involved the issue of slavery and states' rights. Who had the power to control slavery and its expansion into the territories—the federal government or individual states? In the 1860 election, each political party and, therefore, their candidates had the answer to those questions. The Republican Party was represented by the former Illinois representative Abraham Lincoln. Promising not to interfere where slavery currently existed, the Republican platform also pledged not to let the peculiar institution of slavery spread to the territories.

The Constitutional Union Party, composed of former Southern Whigs as well as those who belonged to the Know-Nothing Party, rallied against the expansion of slavery into the territories. Their candidate in the 1860 election was the former U.S. senator from Tennessee John Bell. The Democratic Party, which met in Charleston, South Carolina, was in total disarray. The Southern Democrats wanted a platform that supported the Dred Scott decision as well as the expansion of slavery in the territories. The Northern Democrats knew that it would be impossible to win a single Northern state with such a platform and were adamant in not supporting the expansion of slavery in the territories and refused to adopt the platform. The Southern delegates responded by leaving the convention in disgust, and the convention ended without the adoption of a platform or an official candidate. The party divisions met later in Baltimore but were unable to resolve their sectional differences. As a result, the Democratic Party presented two candidates for president: representing the Northern wing was Illinois representative Stephen A. Douglas, and representing the Southern wing was John Breckenridge, the sitting vice president of the United States as well as Kentucky's senator-elect.

While there were four prominent candidates who were running for the office of president, in the end, only two of the four candidates were relevant to the voters of Maryland. For the average Maryland voter, presidential candidates Breckenridge and Bell proclaimed their support for the Constitution, the Union and the enforcement of law. Those who supported Breckenridge believed that he was the quintessential Southern candidate, and a vote for him was considered to be a vote for the extension of slavery throughout the West. Supporters of Breckenridge used the slogan "Maryland must and will be True to the South."[57] When the final votes were tallied, Breckenridge had edged out Bell to win the state with 42,482 votes to Bell's 41,760 votes.[58] During the presidential election, eventual winner Abraham Lincoln had a total of 2,294 votes out of a total of 9,242 cast in Maryland, receiving only 1 vote in Prince George's County.

Peace Conference of 1861

The election of Abraham Lincoln was the proverbial straw that broke the camel's back for many Southerners, including many Marylanders who associated a Lincoln victory with the abolition of slavery. In a clear renunciation of his election, the Southern states of South Carolina, Mississippi, Florida, Louisiana, Alabama, Georgia and Texas passed ordinances of secession on February 8, 1861, and created the Confederate States of America. In an effort to resolve the outstanding issues regarding slavery, over one hundred political leaders met at the Willard Hotel in Washington, D.C., to resolve the sectional differences before the Republican administration took office. While the political leaders represented fourteen non-slave states and seven slave states, there were no representatives from the states that had already seceded from the Union. The conference modified a compromise proposal that was previously submitted by Kentucky senator John Crittenden during the last session of Congress. This compromise was then rejected by Congress as well as President-Elect Lincoln. The compromise suggested was almost identical to the Crittenden compromise, which proposed that slavery in the territories would be based on extending the Missouri Compromise to the Pacific Ocean. Unfortunately for the nation, the conference was unsuccessful. Those who attended the conference were unable to come up with a solution that satisfied both the Democrat and Republican Parties on the issue of slavery in the territories.

CALLS FOR MARYLAND TO SECEDE

The election of Abraham Lincoln, the secession and subsequent creation of the Confederate States of America, the firing on Fort Sumter, the declaration of war and the Baltimore Riots of 1861 showed the division of Maryland citizens, with southern and western Marylanders calling for Maryland to join the Confederacy and northern Marylanders insisting that Maryland remain within the Union. The Maryland state convention was to be held in March 1861, and Prince George's was to be represented by four delegates. Instead of sending delegates, however, Prince Georgians voted against holding a convention. Newspapers in western and northern Maryland expressed strong support for the Union, and editorials called for Maryland to remain in the Union. In Prince George's County, the sentiment was very different. The *Planter's Advocate*, a weekly newspaper based out of Upper Marlboro, called for Maryland to secede. Upon hearing the news that Prince Georgians voted against holding a secession convention, the newspaper complained

First Blood: Baltimore, taken from the May 4, 1861 issue of *Harper's Weekly*.

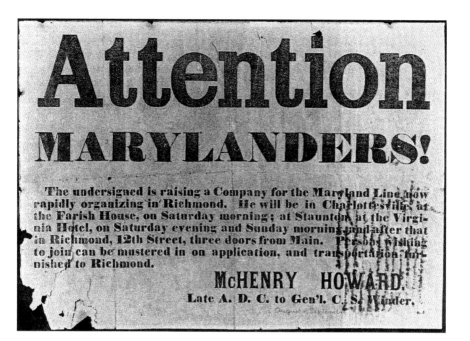

In 1862, McHenry Howard posted this advertisement recruiting Marylanders to join the Maryland Line in the Confederate army. *Maryland State Archives*.

that "the least exertion on the part of the friends of the movement could have elicited a vote that would have overwhelmed the completion."[59] Denied the use of the mails, the *Planter's Advocate* ceased operating in 1861.

Thomas Holliday Hicks served as Maryland's governor from 1858 to 1862. Governor Hicks, a member of the American Nativist Party, or the Know-Nothing Party, was born in Dorchester County. A true man of his times, Governor Hicks viewed slaves as property rather than human beings. In an address to the Maryland General Assembly on January 6, 1860, Governor Hicks stated, "The attacks of fanatical and misguided persons against property in slaves, and the warfare carried on by certain parties in the States north of us, against the rights of citizens in those States which still retain the institution of slavery, were formerly confined to a few; who were forced to content themselves with refusing assistance to, or placing obstacles in the way of, our citizens, who proceeded to those States, under the guarantees of the Constitution, to recover their property."[60] Despite these beliefs, Governor Hicks was a supporter of the Union, and following the secession of the Southern states and the declaration of war, he resisted calls from his constituents to adopt a pro-Southern strategy. Following the election of

Governor Thomas Hicks was forced to hold a special session of the Maryland legislature in Frederick County to decide whether Maryland would secede from the Union. *Library of Congress.*

Lincoln, there was already talk of the Southern states leaving the Union. On December 8, 1860, Governor Hicks wrote a letter to Captain Contee from Prince George's County stating, "If the Union must be dissolved, let it be done calmly, deliberately and after full reflection on the part of the united south. After allowing a reasonable time for action on the part of the northern states, if they shall neglect or refuse to observe the plain requirements of the constitution, then, in my judgment, we shall be fully warranted in demanding a division of the country."[61]

Distrustful of the Democratic legislature who pressured Governor Hicks to adopt a more pro-Southern position, Hicks tried to avoid calling on the legislature to discuss the issue of secession. On January 3, 1861, Governor Hicks issued a "Proclamation to the People of Maryland," which was a formal statement of his views regarding slavery, the Union and Maryland. In his proclamation, Hicks discussed his reasons for not calling a special session of the legislature. He also denounced the Northern evasions of the fugitive slave law and expressed his desire to always live in a slave state.[62] Hicks, however, did not feel that secession was a good idea and hoped to spend the remainder of his days in the Union.

THE CIVIL WAR BEGINS

The Civil War began on April 12, 1861, with the firing on Fort Sumter in South Carolina by Confederate forces. As the nation's capital was surrounded by the Confederate state of Virginia and the border state of Maryland, President

Lincoln called for volunteers to save the Union. Approximately seventy-five thousand volunteer soldiers from Massachusetts and Pennsylvania began making their way to Washington, D.C., by train, first arriving in Baltimore. Waiting for the arrival of these soldiers were citizens who were both Southern sympathizers as well as supporters of the Union. The Southern sympathizers believed that making the South return to the Union by force was a violation of states' rights, and they proceeded to attack the trains with bricks and stones and block their route. In response, some of the troops shot at the crowd. The ensuing tragedy soon included the troops, the Southern sympathizers, Union supporters and Baltimore police. When all was said and done, the dead included four soldiers and twelve civilians. James Ryder Randall, who lost a friend in the Baltimore Riots of 1861, wrote a pro-Southern poem about the event called "Maryland, My Maryland," which offered such lyrics as, "The despot's heel is on thy shore, Maryland! His torch I at thy temple door, Maryland! Avenge the patriotic gore. That flecked the streets of Baltimore. And be the battle queen of yore, Maryland! My Maryland![63] This poem would later be used as a war hymn by the Confederacy and adopted by Maryland as the official state song in 1939.

Despite the bloodshed and continued violence, volunteers would continue to arrive in Baltimore on their way to Washington, D.C. Governor Hicks also appealed to the people of Maryland. At a meeting in Monument Square, Governor Hicks declared, "I am a Marylander. I love my State, and I love the Union!"[64] In an effort to avoid more bloodshed, Governor Hicks and Baltimore mayor George William Brown wrote a letter to President Lincoln requesting that the troops avoid Baltimore and be rerouted to Annapolis, Maryland. Hearing no response, the governor took the unusual step of planning to disable the lines to stop Union troops from arriving in the city. While President Lincoln soon agreed to reroute the troops to Annapolis, he also issued the writ of habeas corpus. Union general Benjamin Butler soon occupied Annapolis, seized the railroads linking the city with Baltimore and on May 13, 1861, seized control of Baltimore.

SPECIAL SESSION OF THE LEGISLATURE

The firing on Fort Sumter and the subsequent declaration of war made the issue of Maryland secession one that could no longer be ignored by Governor Hicks. As the General Assembly met biannually, a special session of the legislature was called on April 22, 1861, by Governor Hicks. The session was originally scheduled to convene in the state capital of Annapolis. On April 24, however, Governor Hicks abruptly changed the location of the meeting to Frederick. While the true reason for the change is not clear, many Marylanders believed that Governor Hicks changed the location from Annapolis, where many favored secession, to Frederick, which was more of a pro-Union town. Nonetheless, because of the sudden change, many representatives from the southern part of the county were unable to make it to the special session. The session was originally scheduled to meet in the Frederick County Courthouse, but because of the large number of participants, the session met in Kemp Hall, the meeting room of the German Reformed Church.[65] The following resolution was immediately offered: "We cannot but know that a large proportion of the citizens of Maryland have been induced to believe that there is a probability that our deliberations may result in the passage of some measure committing this state to secession. It is therefore our duty to declare that all fears are without foundation. We know that we have no constitutional authority to take such action."[66] Among those who supported the resolution was John B. Brooke of Prince George's County.

Despite this binding resolution, a petition calling for the legislature "to pass an Ordinance of Secession without delay" was submitted by the Honorable Edward Pilny Bryan. Representing Prince George's County in the House of Delegates, Bryan was a staunch Confederate supporter and would later show his loyalty to the Southern cause by serving as a spy. While the petition was referred to the Committee of Federal Relations, the committee declined to take any action, as "the legislature does not possess the power to pass such an ordinance as it is prayed."[67] In addition to Bryan and Brooke, Prince George's County was also represented by Richard Wooten and Ethan A. Jones. On April 29, the legislature voted 53–13 against secession. Joining Bryan in voting for secession was Wooten.

During the legislative session, many resolutions were passed calling for the support of the Confederate states. One such resolution was passed by the Maryland Senate on May 14, 1861. The resolution stated that the state of Maryland "earnestly and anxiously desired the restoration of peace between the belligerent sections of the county and the president [of the Confederate Sates of America], authorities and people of the Confederate States, having over and over again officially and unofficially declared that they see only peace and self-defense and to be left alone…that they were willing to throw down the sword. The Senators and Delegates of Maryland do beseech and implore the President of the United States to accept the olive branch which is thus held out to him." While this resolution was passed with no dissent, it had no immediate effect on President Lincoln.[68]

On June 22, 1861, Resolution No. 13 requested that the "Representatives and Senators in Maryland in the Congress of the United States urge and vote for an immediate recognition of the independence of the government of the Confederate States." The resolution was sent to members of Congress, including the Speaker of the House, the president of the Senate and the Maryland representatives in the Senate, John A. Pearce and Anthony Kennedy.[69] This resolution was passed by a vote of 9–3 and included the support of John B. Brooke from Prince George's. In addition, there were numerous correspondences between Federal and state officials requesting the removal of Federal troops from Maryland. These requests were all for naught due to Maryland's logistical position of bordering the Federal city.

GOVERNING DURING THE WAR

A special congressional election was held in June 1861 to determine who would represent Maryland's sixth congressional district in the House of Representatives. Charles Benedict Calvert of Riversdale represented the Union ticket and Benjamin Gwinn Harris of St. Mary's County, the Democratic ticket. Calvert, a slaveholder who descended from the Lords Baltimore, was a Unionist who declared, "If Maryland has grievances under the general government, she should seek a remedy for them in and out of the Union." Calvert believed that no state had the right to secede.[70]

In the fall of 1861, the general election for state and county offices was held. Representing the Union slate for governor was Augustus W. Bradford, while General Benjamin C. Howard represented the Democrats. Bradford was a well-known orator, and both candidates had represented Maryland at the Washington Peace Conference in 1861. The Union party campaigned on the issues of the Union and slavery. In order to ensure support for the Union, Federal troops were dispatched to protect them as they made their ways to the polls. Many of the Maryland secessionists, who supported the Confederate cause and left the state only to return for the election, were held prisoner until the conclusion of the election. Bradford defeated Howard by approximately thirty thousand votes in an election that was marred by the illegal use of troops as well as voter intimidation. Augustus Bradford

Page one of Senator John Bayne's letter to Governor Bradford. *Maryland State Archives.*

took the oath as governor of Maryland on January 8, 1862. Looking to represent Prince George's County in the Maryland House of Delegates were two respected citizens, Dr. John H. Bayne and Oden Bowie. Dr. Bayne, the Unionist candidate, was a respected slave owner and physician who served many people in Prince George's County, including John and Mary Surratt. Despite the fact that Oden Bowie, representing the states' rights ticket, was a respected planter whose plantation, Fairview, was located in

Page two of Senator John Bayne's letter to Governor Bradford. *Maryland State Archives.*

Collington, Maryland, he was defeated by Dr. Bayne. Oden Bowie of Prince George's was part of a group of prominent legislators who met in Annapolis to reestablish the state Democratic Party and was a delegate at the 1864 Democratic National Convention.

These two elections showed the dichotomy that existed in Prince George's County during the early days of the war. As the Unionist candidates came from long-standing, respected and, in many instances, slave-owning families,

Site of the 1861 special session of the Maryland General Assembly in Frederick, Maryland. *Library of Congress.*

they were rewarded by winning their elections. While there was tremendous support for the South in Prince George's County, there was also loyalty to the North. As long as slavery was not threatened, many believed that there was no need for Maryland to secede; thus, the Unionists were often victorious in the elections. As it became evident that Maryland would not join the South in seceding from the Union, many Prince Georgians left their homes and farms and joined the Confederate army. In September 1861, twenty-seven legislators were charged as being disloyal and pro-Southern. They were released only after pledging their oaths of allegiance to the Union.

EMANCIPATION PROCLAMATION

On January 1, 1863, the Emancipation Proclamation was issued by President Lincoln. The Emancipation Proclamation freed the slaves in the Confederate states as well as the states occupied by Federal troops. While the proclamation had no legal authority in Maryland, discussion was already underway among the Maryland Unionists to dissolve the practice of slavery in the state. In April 1863, a group of Maryland politicians meeting at the Maryland Institute of Baltimore supported compensated emancipation in the state. This meeting was attended by Governor Thomas Hicks, Montgomery Blair and future governor August Bradford.

During the interim between the Emancipation Proclamation and the Constitutional Convention of 1864, legislation was submitted to the Maryland General Assembly to end slavery in Maryland. An example included a motion submitted by Peregrine Davis of Charles County on January 11, 1864, requesting that a special committee be allowed to introduce legislation that would voluntarily emancipate the slaves as well as compensate the owners for the loss of their property. It was resolved that the members of the U.S. Congress would be requested to secure a law "whereby all loyal owners may be compensated for the loss of their slaves." Several revisions were submitted, including one that removed the term "loyal owners" and inserted "all who own slaves and have not engaged in actual hostilities against the government of the United States or given aid and comfort to those engaged in hostilities against the said government."[71] While the amendments were rejected, the final bill passed by a vote of 52–15. A similar amendment was proposed in the Maryland State Senate and also failed to garner the necessary votes. Further legislation was passed on February 17, 1864, by the Maryland Senate by a vote of 13–6 calling for the "compensation of all loyal citizens of Maryland whose property had been taken, damaged or destroyed by the armies of the United States or the so-called Confederate States." Among those who dissented was John H. Bayne of Prince George's County.

Although the Union Party exerted control of the Maryland state government, in the southern counties of Prince George's, St. Mary's and Charles, the Democratic Party remained the true power player. After the Emancipation Proclamation, in the 1863 election for the House of Representatives, Democrat Benjamin Gwinn Harris of St. Mary's County, who advocated secession, defeated incumbent Charles Benedict Calvert of Prince George's County, who despite being a supporter of slave owner's property rights was the Unionist candidate.

CONSTITUTIONAL CONVENTION OF 1864

As the war progressed, the belief that slaves should be freed gathered steam among Maryland abolitionists and the unconditional Union politicians, particularly after President Lincoln issued the Emancipation Proclamation. This proclamation, however, was in direct contrast with the Maryland Constitution that passed in 1851, but as the Maryland Unionists had control of the state government, they began to make overtures in seeking to change the constitution. The issue of slavery in Maryland was finally put to rest in April 1864. A constitutional convention was convened by Governor Bradford on April 27, 1864, to discuss the issue of freeing Maryland slaves either with or without compensating their owners, as well as the future of slavery in Maryland. At the convention, Prince George's County was represented by Daniel Clarke, Samuel H. Berry and Edward Belt. Daniel Clarke recommended that as a condition of freeing Maryland slaves on January 1, 1865, the U.S. Congress should compensate the slave owners for the loss of their personal property. As a part of this recommendation, Clarke also called for the appropriation of $20 million to reimburse slave owners.[72] The total emancipation of slaves was approved by a vote of 57–27. The idea of compensating slave owners was soundly defeated by the Unionist majority.

In addition to abolishing slavery in the state, the Maryland Constitution of 1864 also disenfranchised those who not only fought in the Confederate army and navy but also those private citizens who expressed support for the Southern cause. In order to regain the right to vote, the disenfranchised had to take an oath of allegiance to the State of Maryland and the United States of America as well as repudiate the rebellion. The new constitution also altered the legislative makeup of the Maryland General Assembly by limiting the power of the smaller counties that previously had large slave populations. The Constitution of 1864 was passed by a vote of 53–26, with 17 abstaining from voting. The constitution was ratified by a vote of 30,174–29,799 on October 13, 1864. Prince George's County citizens showed their disdain by voting 1,293 against the law versus the 149 who supported it.[73] The election results were again marred by concerns of fraud and voter intimidation. Former Confederate soldiers from Maryland were not given the opportunity to vote, whereas Union soldiers from Maryland supported the new constitution by a vote of 2,633–263.[74]

During the 1864 presidential election, incumbent president Abraham Lincoln defeated the Democratic candidate General George McClellan. Lincoln won the state of Maryland and its 7 electoral votes by beating McClellan 40,153–32,739.[75]

On February 1, 1865, the Thirteenth Amendment to the constitution was sent to Annapolis for ratification. This amendment outlawed slavery in the United States. In a speech before both Houses of the legislature, Governor Bradford urged the lawmakers to support the amendment. While the amendment passed the House of Delegates with no significant issue, it passed the state senate by a vote of 11–10.[76] Among those who declined to ratify the amendment was Daniel Clarke of Prince George's County.

Chapter 5

Secret Lines of Allegiance

D uring the Civil War, Marylanders were deeply divided over whether the state should pledge loyalty to the Union or the Confederacy. The state's geographical position made it very important to the Union. If Maryland seceded to the Confederacy, Washington, D.C., would be surrounded by enemy territory and cut off from communication with the North. Even though the state ended up not seceding, most Prince George's County citizens were Confederate sympathizers.[77] The county's population was so devoted to the Southern cause that only one person in Prince George's County voted for Abraham Lincoln in the 1860 presidential election.[78] The leaders of social and public life in Prince George's County were all slave owners.[79] The county had the most slaves in the state, and its economy relied heavily on its tobacco fields and plantations. Therefore, the county had more to lose than any other in Maryland if the Union prevailed in the Civil War because it needed its slave labor to keep its economy going. Many Prince Georgians joined Confederate military forces, developed a smuggling and spy line to the South or engaged in underground activities.[80]

CONFEDERATE SYMPATHIES

Although Prince George's County citizens were sympathetic to the South, most did not actually want Maryland to secede. The county was a

Civil War recruitment poster. *Library of Congress, Prints and Photographs Division.*

conservative area, and seceding from the Union would be a major change. In addition, the county would almost definitely become a battleground if Maryland seceded because of its proximity to Washington, D.C. Some strong opponents to the Union advocated secession, but the county voted against it in three elections. Prince Georgians basically wanted to keep the institution of slavery without separating from the United States.[81] Despite that, the area had its share of rebellious activity brought on by supporters of the Confederacy. Those discovered were arrested and freed only after signing an oath of allegiance to the Union. Many young men in Prince George's County who supported the South left the area to enlist in the Confederate army, believing they would likely be drafted into the Union army if they stayed.[82] One of these men was a member of the Snowden family, who built the mill on which Laurel, Maryland, is based. Nicholas Snowden, grandson of Major Thomas Snowden of Montpelier in the northern part of the county, traveled with friends William K. Howard and Mason E. McKnew for several days to Harpers Ferry to join the Confederate army in May 1860. Taking the oath of allegiance on June 1, 1861, Nicholas earned the rank of third lieutenant in Company D under the command of Captain James Rawlings Herbert of the First Maryland Infantry Battalion. Nicholas died at the age of thirty-two in the Battle of Port Republic in Harrisonburg, Virginia, on June 6, 1862.[83]

In early 1861, the Southern states were holding conventions to decide whether they would stay in the Union or secede to the Confederacy. Maryland was supposed to hold a state convention, with Prince George's County sending four delegates, but the county voted by a narrow margin against holding such a convention. Slavery was not an issue in the first year of the Civil War, which was more about the rebellion of the Southern states. At that point, the government promised to allow Maryland to keep slavery if it remained in the Union, and Prince George's citizens were satisfied to stay under that condition.[84]

The Union, however, was criticized by Prince George's County newspapers the *Marlboro Gazette* and the *Planters' Advocate*. Published by George W. Wilson, the *Marlboro Gazette* printed a column of war news entitled "Progress of the Second War of Independence."[85] The paper was denied distribution by mail because of its Confederate leanings and had to suspend publication during the war.[86] The paper, however, was reborn as *The Prince Georgian* a few months later.[87] Wilson was imprisoned for a brief period in 1862 at the Old Capitol Prison in Washington, D.C., for denouncing Federal draft laws, according to a note in a January 6, 1882 issue of *The Prince Georgian*.[88] Thomas J. Turner, publisher of the *Planters' Advocate*, promoted slavery many years before the war broke out. In an article printed on November 12, 1851, Thomas stated:

> *The bickering, jealousies and ill-will between North and South will continue so long as the institution of slavery which we cherish continues to be misunderstood by true men and misrepresented by fanatics. It is not sufficient, therefore, that we convince ourselves of its justice and utility. It becomes our duty to convince others also, that we may claim forbearance at their hands and regard for our rights. Thinking thus we should be recreant to our duty did we not endeavor, when occasion served, to throw whatever of light is in our power upon this much vexed subject.*[89]

During the war, Turner blamed the defeat of states' rights in the election on the presence of Federal troops and "corrupting influences brought to bear from the Capital" in Prince George's County and several other Maryland counties such as Howard and Montgomery. According to Turner, two polling places were near Union camps, and two others were near Union fortresses. In a column about the recent election, printed on June 19, 1861, he wrote, "The States' Rights men had refused to make an open contest, under the pressure of Federal bayonets."[90] In the same column, he stated:

> *From Fort Washington, up the Potomac, and along the upper line of the county, the military control was evident—and coupled with numerous rumors of intended interference, not only prevented a full turn-out of the people, but, we have no doubt, affected the course of many who did vote. In Montgomery County, Mr. Calvert gets nearly a thousand majorities—a figure so monstrously out of proportion to the well-known divisions of public sentiment, as to show at once that such a result could only have been caused by the almost entire non-action of his opponents. The same remark applies to Howard and to this county. Apart from this, even where the States' Rights cause was strongest, the efforts in its behalf appear to have been the least.*[91]

Like the *Marlboro Gazette*, the *Planter's Advocate* was banned from the mail during the war, and Turner eventually fled the area to escape arrest by Federal authorities.[92]

Prince Georgians' support shifted from the Union to the Confederacy as the war continued on longer than expected and became bloodier and bloodier. Once the Lincoln administration began to advocate abolitionism as the solution to the conflict, the Prince George's County government was taken over in the local elections in 1863 by officials who were strongly opposed to Lincoln and the war effort.[93]

A NETWORK OF SPIES

Prince George's County was a strategic spot for secret Confederate affairs. Many in the county worked hard to subvert the Union's efforts to keep travel and communication lines to and from Washington, D.C., open. Protecting the area's routes of travel and communication was critical to the Federal government remaining effective during the war.[94] Of course, the Confederacy also wanted to protect its own routes for sending information. Many Prince Georgians worked together to create spy networks throughout the county that were used to pass information from Washington, D.C., to Richmond, Virginia. These spy networks ran through the Northern Neck of Virginia into Charles County, Maryland, and through southern Prince George's County into the District.[95] A line of communication that ran through Upper Marlboro was important to the Confederacy. Even though it was actually controlled by Federal troops, Confederate agents found ways to operate undetected.[96] Some Prince George's citizens waited at obscure points along the Potomac River with boats to take Southern agents across. Confederate sympathizers hung a dress or shirt as if to dry in order to let agents hidden along the shore know whether the Union watch was close or inattentive.[97] At these crossing points, agents took recruits and mail across the river and brought back spies and top-secret communications from Richmond for Rebel agents operating as far north as Canada.[98] John Wilkes Booth used the secret routes through the county to learn the country roads and develop details of his conspiracy plot against President Lincoln.[99]

The Confederacy's spy network had many connections in Prince George's County through the owners and families of large agricultural farms and plantations. Active Confederate agents lived in villages throughout the county such as Woodville (now Aquasco), T.B., Piscataway, Upper Marlboro and Surrattsville (which will be further discussed later). Federal forces frequently raided plantations and homes in these areas looking for weapons and supplies that were to be shipped to the South.[100] Early in the war, a cavalry unit made up of more than two hundred soldiers conducted a late nighttime raid on Mount Auburn, home of Bennett Gwynn, near Surrattsville. Gwynn Park, home of William H. Gwynn in T.B., frequently had its meat house raided. Just a few miles away, Pleasant Springs, Captain Andrew J. Gwynn's home, was burned down because the Federal government believed his wife was accepting and moving secret enemy mail while he was away fighting for the Confederacy. The home was also suspected to be a safe house for Confederate agents. Legend has it that Union soldiers paid a family slave to set the fire.[101] E. Pliny Bryan, a well-known staunch Confederate supporter who lived on the banks of the Potomac River in Accokeek, was another Prince George's County citizen participating in espionage activities against the Union. Bryan went to Charleston to help mine a harbor with torpedoes. He died there in 1864 after contracting yellow fever.[102]

Walter Bowie, of Upper Marlboro, was one of the most daring soldiers and spies for the Confederacy. Bowie made frequent raids into Maryland to both undermine the Union and obtain vital information. On one excursion, he was captured and imprisoned in the Old Capitol Prison in Washington, D.C., and condemned to be shot. Bowie escaped on the night before his planned execution by climbing to the roof while the guard was asleep and climbing down a rainspout to reach the ground. He joined a group of friends who were waiting with a horse and made it to Virginia. On another trip into Maryland, Union soldiers chased Walter Bowie to the plantation of his kinsman, John Henry Waring, in Prince George's County. He was completely surrounded but used his resourcefulness to escape. Waring's daughter helped Bowie blacken his face and dress as a female servant. With a bandana around his head and an empty milk pail under his arm, he made it past his would-be captors by pretending to be on an errand to get water from a nearby spring.[103] Instead, he retrieved his horse and rode away to safety.[104] During yet another raid in Maryland, Bowie was once again chased by Union soldiers when he made it to a plantation in an isolated section of northern Prince George's County near the Patuxent River. The plantation was owned by Confederate sympathizer and slave owner Francis Newman. He reused one of his previous tactics and donned one of Mrs. Newman's wrappers, a huge sunbonnet with a string tied under his chin. He made it through a squadron of soldiers carrying a basket of eggs and several live chickens.[105]

Thomas Harbin, who lived in Piscataway, and Augustus Howell were two other Prince Georgians involved in espionage for the Confederacy. Howell often escorted female couriers between Richmond and the "Confederate

Cabinet" in Canada. Both Harbin and Howell later worked with John Surratt Jr., the most famous Confederate agent from the county. Surratt's skill in eluding Union troops led to an introduction to John Wilkes Booth and involvement in a plot to kidnap President Abraham Lincoln.[106]

THE CONSPIRATORS' PLOT

After the Federal government passed the Emancipation Proclamation in early 1863, the defenses of Washington, D.C., began to relax, and the Confederate spy networks were brought down. Even though the Emancipation Proclamation did not free slaves in Maryland, many in Prince George's County saw the president as a threat to their livelihood. When slavery was abolished in Maryland by a new state constitution enacted on November 1, 1864, the county's Confederate sympathizers were enraged. Among them were the family of John and Mary Surratt, who were involved in what is probably the county's most infamous story of treachery against the Union. The Surratts took part in the conspiracy plot that eventually led to the assassination of Abraham Lincoln.[107]

John Harrison Surratt met Mary Jenkins in 1839, when he was twenty-six and she was seventeen, and they were married in August 1840.[108] Only a few details are known about John's background, including that he was a heavy drinker and gambler. He fathered one child out of wedlock before he met Mary.[109] Also, he inherited a portion of a farm in Washington, D.C., from his wealthy adoptive parents, Richard and Sarah Neale.[110] For the first few years of their marriage, John and Mary Surratt lived at a mill in Oxon Hill, Maryland, and then on John's inherited farmland. While there, they had three children: Isaac, born in 1841; Elizabeth Susanna "Anna," born in 1843; and John Jr., born in 1844.[111] A fire destroyed the farmhouse in 1851; an escaped family slave was suspected of setting the blaze.[112] Within a year, John bought two hundred acres of farmland located near a crossroads in an area of Prince George's County that was twelve miles from Washington, D.C., and just a few miles from where Mary Surratt grew up.[113] John Surratt opened a tavern and public dining room in two rooms of his home. Surratt also offered a sleeping space upstairs for twenty-five cents a night, while a livery stable and blacksmith shop across the road provided extra services to travelers and neighbors. The tavern was a popular way station for travelers coming from Virginia to D.C. because it was so close to the District. The town—now known as Clinton—was named "Surrattsville" after a post office

A woodprint depicting Surrattsville and the Surratts' tavern and post office, printed in an 1867 issue of *Harper's Weekly*. *Courtesy of the Surratt House Museum.*

was opened there. John Surratt served as the first postmaster.[114] By 1854, the tavern had become a popular gathering place for local men who would discuss the major issues dividing Maryland and the United States.[115]

Like many of their neighbors, John and Mary Surratt were slave owners and had as many as seven slaves.[116] The Surratts were also Confederate sympathizers, as were other middle-class slaveholders in the county.[117] The Surratt tavern was a hub for secessionist activity by the late 1850s. John Surratt was a vocal secessionist at the beginning of the Civil War, and the Surratt home became a safe house in the county's Confederate spy network.[118] The government suspected that secessionist activities were taking place at the Surratt tavern and had its eye on John Surratt. His son Isaac left the county on Inauguration Day in 1861 and fought throughout the war as part of a Texas cavalry unit.[119] The Surratt family was left in debt after John Surratt died suddenly in the summer of 1862. John Surratt Jr., who was attending the seminary at St. Charles College, left school and returned home to run the family's farm and post office.[120] He also served as a courier and spy for the Confederate Secret Service, carrying secret mail detailing Union troop movements across the Potomac River, between Richmond and Confederate exiles in Canada.[121] Surratt lost his position as postmaster when the government discovered his role as a courier for the Confederacy. It is unknown how he managed to avoid arrest, but he was left with more time for his espionage activities.[122]

John H. Surratt Jr., son of Mary Surratt, acted as a courier and spy for the Confederate army after the death of his father. *Library of Congress, Prints and Photographs Division.*

With her husband dead and sons away, Mary Surratt struggled to keep the family farm, tavern and other businesses running. Located within Union lines, the tavern suffered financial losses due to attacks from Union soldiers.[123] Also, a number of the family's slaves escaped to freedom after slavery was abolished in Washington, D.C., in 1862, adding to the burden on Mary and her daughter. In the fall of 1864, Mary Surratt decided to rent out her home in Prince George's County and move to a boardinghouse the family owned in D.C.[124] She rented the home, tavern and farm to John Lloyd, a former D.C. police officer and Confederate sympathizer. Lloyd acted as innkeeper and did some farming on the land. Mary Surratt moved into the three-story boardinghouse in October 1864 and, once established, began taking in boarders, including Louis Weichmann.

Because of his expertise in evading Union troops, John Surratt Jr. came to the attention of a group of Confederate sympathizers who were plotting against President Abraham Lincoln.[125] Led by popular actor John Wilkes Booth, the group planned to kidnap Lincoln, move him into Richmond through southern Prince George's County and Charles County and exchange him for thousands of Confederate prisoners of war. Dr. Samuel A. Mudd, a physician from Charles County, introduced Surratt and Booth at the National Hotel in Washington, D.C., on December 23, 1864. Although he was initially suspicious of Booth, John Surratt Jr. agreed to aid in the plot once he learned the full extent of it. Booth and other members of his gang became frequent visitors of Mary Surratt's boardinghouse between the winter of 1864 and the spring of 1865.[126] Lewis Powell, one of the conspirators, often went to the house disguised as a minister. Booth frequently traveled to the country, likely scouting the route the conspirators planned to use in the kidnapping.[127]

The kidnapping attempt took place on March 17, 1865, when Booth learned that the president was planning to attend a performance of the play *Still Waters Run Deep* at Campbell General Hospital near the Soldier's Home. John Surratt Jr., Booth and the other conspirators hid on a stretch of road near the Soldier's Home, waiting for the president's carriage en route to the hospital.[128] The carriage never appeared, and Booth later learned that the president changed his plans at the last minute to attend a reception at the National Hotel, which coincidentally was where Booth was staying. The conspirators hid rifles, ammunition and other supplies at the Surratt tavern following the failed kidnapping attempt.[129]

The conspirators' plot soon evolved from kidnapping to murder. Booth shot President Lincoln at Ford's Theatre in Washington, D.C., on the night of April 14, 1865. After breaking his leg in a leap onto the stage from the presidential box, Booth met up with accomplice David E. Herold and fled the city. Booth and Herold rode straight to the Surratt home in Prince George's County and stopped briefly to retrieve items they had left at the property.[130] Herold entered the tavern and returned with the items, which included field glasses (binoculars) that allegedly belonged to Booth.[131] The pair then rode to Mudd's home in Charles County, where Mudd treated Booth's broken leg. Booth and Herold continued south to the Potomac River and the Northern Neck of Virginia.[132] Federal troops trapped Booth in a barn in Caroline County, Virginia, on April 26, 1865, and demanded he surrender. They set the barn on fire when Booth refused. A soldier fatally shot Booth in the back of his neck after taking aim through the cracks in the barn. Booth was dragged onto the porch of a nearby farmhouse, where he died within a few hours.[133]

The authorities sought out John Surratt Jr. in connection with Lincoln's assassination once it became clear that he had connections to Booth and was somehow involved in the conspiracy.[134] Surratt was one of the first people suspected of an attack on Secretary of State William H. Seward that took place at the same time as Lincoln's assassination. However, it was soon discovered that Lewis Powell was behind the attempted murder of Seward.[135] Surratt later claimed he was on Confederate assignment in Elmira, New York, at the time of the assassination and denied any involvement in the murder plot. Unaware that John Surratt Jr. had left the area, the Metropolitan police went to Mary Surratt's home looking for her son. Union army officials interrogated Mary a few days later, on April 17, 1865, and searched her home for evidence; they found images of Confederate generals and items that implicated her as a Southern

Campbell General Hospital in Washington, D.C. *Library of Congress, Prints and Photographs Division.*

sympathizer. Powell came to the home while the army officials were at the boardinghouse, and both were arrested. Mary was taken to the Old Capitol Prison before being transferred to the Washington Arsenal Penitentiary. The Union army alleged that she assisted, or at least knew of, Booth's assassination plot.[136]

Mary Surratt and seven other conspirators—Powell, Herold, Mudd, Michael O'Laughlen, Edman Spangler, Samuel Arnold and George A. Atzerodt—went on trial by court-martial the next month. Surratt's tenant, John Lloyd, was also arrested and charged in the conspiracy. Lloyd was kept in solitary confinement until he agreed to testify against Surratt. Lloyd said John Surratt Jr., Atzerodt and Herold visited the tavern and asked him to hide a pair of carbines, ammunition, rope and a wrench and that he and John Surratt Jr. hid the package in the ceiling above the tavern's main dining room on March 18. Lloyd testified that Mary Surratt went to the tavern on April 11 and told him to have guns ready to be picked up. Lloyd, who was eventually set free, also testified that she made another visit on the afternoon of the assassination and gave him a package containing field glasses to give to Booth that night. She again told him to have guns ready for pick up.[137] Mary, however, claimed she made the trips to collect debts.[138] In addition to Lloyd's testimony, several residents at the boardinghouse said that Surratt regularly met with Booth and the other conspirators at the D.C. residence.[139] Louis Weichmann was another crucial witness against Mary Surratt. Weichmann testified that he went with Mary to the tavern on the day of the assassination and witnessed her leaving the package that Booth and Herold later retrieved. Weichmann also said that Surratt met with Booth at least three times on the same day. Spy and courier Augustus Howell, who also spent time at Mary's boardinghouse, testified against her at the trial as well.

Satisfied that she was guilty of having prior knowledge of the assassination, the military court found Mary and the seven alleged conspirators guilty. Mudd, O'Laughlen, Spangler and Arnold each received a prison sentence, while Mary Surratt, Powell, Herold and Atzerodt were sentenced to death.[140] On the afternoon of July 7, 1865, Surratt climbed the steps of the scaffold at the Washington Arsenal Penitentiary. Her wrists, arms and legs were then bound. A white hanging hood was placed over Mary Surratt's head, and she stood beside Powell, Herold and Atzerodt. Once the signal was given, the scaffold fell, and Mary Surratt became the first woman executed by the United States government.[141] Although Mary was vilified by the press and the public during the seven-week trial, many expressed horror after the execution. Despite the testimony, many have doubted Mary Surratt's involvement in the crime, and it is still debated to this day. At the time of her death, a case was pending before the U.S. Supreme Court questioning the jurisdiction of military courts in cases involving civilians. Less

Secretary of State William H. Seward was attacked at the same time President Lincoln was assassinated. *National Archives and Records Administration.*

Lewis Powell, one of the conspirators convicted of aiding in John Wilkes Booth's assassination plot, standing in an overcoat with a Federal guard to the left. *Library of Congress, Prints and Photographs Division.*

than a year after Surratt's execution, the Supreme Court ruled that a military court had no jurisdiction in civilian cases if the civil courts were open. If this were true when Surratt was convicted, she would have had a different trial and may not have been found guilty.

John Surratt Jr. was still at large during his mother's trial. Surratt was hidden by friends in Canada during the summer and then boarded a steamer headed for Liverpool, England. He later traveled to Italy, where, under the assumed name John Watson, he enlisted in the Papal

Lewis Powell seated and manacled. *Library of Congress, Prints and Photographs Division.*

Zouaves—an infantry force that protected the Papal States. A former acquaintance recognized him, and with his identity revealed, Surratt fled to Egypt. He was captured there and brought back to the United States for trial in early 1867.

Surratt faced numerous trials before being set free more than a year later.[142] The first trial began on June 10, 1867, in the District of Columbia City Hall and was conducted by the Criminal Court of the District of Columbia. Surratt was charged with complicity in the assassination of President Lincoln. The prosecutors—District Attorney Edward Carrington and his assistant, Nathaniel Wilson—argued Surratt's guilt on the basis

The four condemned conspirators—Mary Surratt, Lewis Powell, David Herold and George Atzerodt—at the Washington Arsenal Penitentiary with officers and others on the scaffold and guards on the wall. *Library of Congress, Prints and Photographs Division.*

Opposite, top: The hanging, hooded bodies of the four conspirators with the crowd departing. *Library of Congress, Prints and Photographs Division.*

Opposite, bottom: The grave of Mary Surratt at the Mount Olivet Cemetery in Washington. *Library of Congress, Prints and Photographs Division.*

that he frequently associated with Booth, mainly using the testimony of Louis Weichmann as evidence.[143] They also tried to prove that John Surratt Jr. was in the District when the crime occurred. Several witnesses testified that they saw Surratt in Washington, D.C., on the day of the assassination. Two of the witnesses, however, conceded that they had been paid for their testimony. The prosecution also argued that the guilty verdict in Mary Surratt's trial proved her son was guilty as well. Despite the prosecution's attempts to prove Surratt participated in the crime, the jury failed to come up with a verdict. Surratt sat in jail for a year before his next trial. It was not until June 1868 that a grand jury indicted Surratt on a second charge

of participating in a conspiracy by giving aid and comfort to the enemy, which was punishable by ten years in jail or a fine of $10,000. Surratt pleaded not guilty on June 22, 1868—four days after the charges were filed. He was released on bail the same day, and no action was taken on the case that summer. John Surratt filed a special plea on September 22, 1868, asking for dismissal on grounds that he was included in a general pardon issued by President Andrew Johnson on July 4 of that year. The

John H. Surratt Jr. in his Papal Zouaves uniform. *Library of Congress, Prints and Photographs Division.*

court dismissed the case against John Surratt Jr. on November 5, 1868.[144] He had escaped prosecution with the same evidence that sent his mother to her death.

Chapter 6

Slavery

When the first Confederate shot was fired at Union forces at Fort Sumter, South Carolina, the institution of slavery had been alive and well for over two hundred years in the state of Maryland. While there is no definitive proof, it is assumed that the first Africans who arrived in the colony of Maryland in 1634 were indentured servants rather than slaves for life. Within the next twenty-five years, legislation was passed by the Maryland General Assembly that soon ended the notion that an African slave could work as an indentured servant for a specified term and then earn his or her freedom at the end of that term. The growth of tobacco as a cash crop, as well as the need for cheap labor, contributed to the growth of slavery in Maryland. While the practice of slavery existed in the entire state of Maryland, it was more prevalent in the southern counties of Prince George's, Charles and St. Mary's, as well as the Eastern Shore. When the war first began, Prince George's County had the largest slave population in Maryland, and its slave owners fought to retain the status quo throughout the conflict. The war's conclusion found the former slaves and slave owners attempting to find balance in the new world order that now existed in Prince George's County. In order to understand the role of slavery in Maryland during the Civil War, it is essential to understand the evolution of slavery in the years preceding the war.

THE INTRODUCTION OF SLAVES IN MARYLAND

The introduction of slaves to Maryland occurred in 1634 with the arrival of blacks in the English province of St. Mary's City. In October 1634, Father Andrew White and another Jesuit priest came to the New World by way of the *Ark* and *Dove* sailing vessels. Accompanying Father White was a mulatto servant named Mathias de Sousa and another servant named Francisco.[145] It is believed that these first blacks were not slaves but rather indentured servants serving with fixed contractual terms like many other indentured servants during the seventeenth century. Until their arrival, labor in the colonies had been provided by the colonists themselves and indentured servants. Indentured servants were often poor young men and women from England who pledged to provide labor for a certain number of years in lieu of monetary wages for passage to the American colonies. Given the opportunity to learn a specific trade, these indentured servants was also fed, clothed and given shelter. Similar to slavery, an indentured servant could be sold from owner to owner and forced to work under less than ideal circumstances. Unlike slaves, however, indentured servants could be paid a small fee upon the completion of their contract and, more importantly, gain their freedom. The demand for white labor began to decline during the 1660s as the wages of servants began to increase, and with the recovering English economy, there was a decline in the number of immigrants, as well as the desire to keep labor costs to a minimum.

The arrival of the first blacks in Maryland led to more questions than answers. Blacks were considered by many white colonists to be inferior to whites. So what should the colony do with blacks? After meeting the terms and conditions of a contract between an indentured servant and a master, the servant was freed, and the master found himself in the position of seeking new labor to replace the freed servant. As there was no legal contract between the master and the slave, there was no danger of the master dealing with the need to find new labor. In 1661, a law was passed by the Maryland General Assembly that forbade marriage between whites and blacks, describing the marriages "always to the Satisfaction of their Lascivious and Lustful desires and to the disgrace not only of the English" married slaves, thus inconveniencing courts and masters with legal debates over the status of the offspring. Also, any free woman so marrying after the act's passage was to serve her husband's master during her husband's lifetime. To further discourage such unions, the children born out of such marriages were to serve their parents' masters until they reached the age of thirty-one.[146] Until overturned by a 1664 law, if a slave was found to have accepted Christianity by way of a baptism, he or she would be freed from slavery by a colonial court.[147] Bowing to the pressure of slave owners stung by the loss of their property, the colonial government took the necessary steps to clear up any and all legal ambiguity regarding slaves. In 1664, "An Act Concerning Negroes and Other Slaves," passed by the colonial government, removed any legal ambiguity by making slaves as well as their children slaves for life.[148]

SLAVERY IN MARYLAND

While slavery was a common in all of Maryland, it was more prevalent in the southern counties and Maryland's Eastern Shore. Many whites who supported the notion of slavery believed that blacks were intellectually inferior to whites and could not provide for themselves without the assistance of whites. The white farmer with a small to medium-size farm aspired to be the slave owner with the large plantation. There were also many whites who insisted that blacks were, in fact, happy to be slaves. The slave marketplace that also served the county was located in the county seat of Upper Marlboro. In 1790, the slave population in Prince George's County was 11,176. It later witnessed a decline to 9,189 in 1810 and a resurgence of 12,479 slaves in 1860.[149] Prince George's County, in fact, had more slaves than any other county in Maryland. The slave population of Maryland was not the only segment that witnessed a population growth in the years following the introduction of slaves to Maryland. In 1790, the population of free blacks in Prince George's County consisted of 164 persons and had grown to 1,198 persons by 1860.[150] According to the Eighth Census of the United States, by 1860, Maryland was the home to 83,942 free blacks and 87,009 slaves.[151] Many whites in the state were uncomfortable with the large number of blacks (both those who were free and those who were slaves) in the state. The growth of freed blacks was contributed to slaves purchasing their freedom, as well as some slaves gaining their freedom after the deaths of their owners.

In an attempt to deal with the increasing number of freed slaves, in 1753, the Maryland General Assembly passed legislation that prohibited any slave owner from voluntarily manumitting or freeing his slaves. In addition, Maryland also passed a law in 1783 that prohibited the importation of slaves into the state.[152] Existing owners who currently owned slaves were exempt

$50 Reward.

RANAWAY from the subscriber, living near the Brick Church, in the Forest of Prince George's County, Maryland, on Tuesday, the 16th of September, 1856, negro man BEN, commonly called

BENJAMIN DUCKETT.

I purchased him from Mr. Edmund B. Duvall, who owns his father. His mother belongs to Mr. Marcus Du Val, near Buena Vista Post Office, in this county; and he, no doubt, may be found in that neighborhood.

BEN is of a dark ginger color, about twenty-five years of age, five feet ten or eleven inches high; has an impediment in his speech, and when spoken to has a down look and pats his left foot. His clothing not recollected, as he has various kinds.

I will give the above reward for his apprehension—no matter where taken—provided he is brought home or secured in jail, so that I get him again.

ZACHARIAH BERRY of Washington.
October 1, 1856—tf

Zachariah Berry, slaveholder and Confederate sympathizer, offered a fifty-dollar reward for a runaway slave. *Maryland State Archives.*

from the law, but any slaves who came to the state to be sold after the law was passed were to be freed. Little by little, the General Assembly passed legislation that restricted freed blacks in Maryland. In 1802, the Maryland General Assembly prohibited the voting rights of free black men. According to Barbara Mills in *"Got My Mind Set on Freedom": Maryland's Story of White and Black Activism*, the legislature also attempted at various time to pass laws that would exclude blacks from holding certain jobs, claiming that they were "economically injurious to white workers."[153] These attempts were ultimately unsuccessful. Freed slaves also had to worry about being captured by overzealous slave hunters. The Fugitive Slave Acts of 1793 and 1850 empowered slave hunters to seize and accuse any black of being an escaped slave and barred the seized black from testifying in court.

THE IMPORTANCE OF TOBACCO

Virginia Geiger, in "Maryland, My Maryland," notes that in the years prior to the Civil War, Maryland's agriculture had settled into a regional pattern: the Eastern Shore and western Maryland were grain-producing areas, southern Maryland cultivated tobacco and the areas around Baltimore and Washington, D.C., specialized in truck gardening and dairying.[154] One could also be forgiven for thinking that the phrase "Tobacco Is King" is and was applicable only to the Southern states, as the commonly used phrase applied to Prince George's County as well. The soil of Prince George's County was ideal for the planting of corn, wheat and, of course, tobacco. In 1860, Prince George's County produced 13 million pounds of tobacco—nearly double that of the nearby counties of Charles and Anne Arundel. *Slavery in the Colonial Chesapeake* notes that cultivation of tobacco required careful, painstaking effort. The seedbed had to be correctly prepared and spaced, as the seedlings could easily be damaged when they were transplanted to the fields. These fragile plants demanded constant care with continual hoeing and weeding. Additional care was needed in worming and topping each plant, cutting the stalks and curing the leaves in the tobacco houses.[155] For the slaves, the work was tedious, grueling and exhausting. However, working in the tobacco fields was not the only chore that occupied the daily life of a slave. Slaves also devoted a considerable amount of their time to clearing out new fields, raising livestock and growing edible crops such as corn and wheat, which eventually began to replace tobacco.

Tobacco commanded such a dominating presence in Maryland's colonial economy that it soon became a medium of exchange. Taxes were assessed, debts paid and land priced not in pounds sterling but in pounds of tobacco. When the tobacco market was good, everyone in the county (with the exception of the slaves) prospered. When it was bad, it was bad. The importance and growth of tobacco had a significant impact on the need for labor, which is why Prince George's County had the largest slave population in the state.

Tobacco was the main crop worked by slaves in Prince George's County. *Library of Congress, Prints and Photographs Division.*

THE LIFE OF A SLAVE

While the day-to-day life of a slave varied from plantation to plantation, what didn't vary was the lack of control that the slave had in his or her personal destiny. Most slaves worked every day from sun up to sun down with the exception of Sunday and maybe a holiday. In a majority of the Southern states, it was illegal for slaves to learn to read and/or write and illegal to teach them. While this was not the case in Maryland, the educating of slaves was nonetheless discouraged. As a result, what is known about the day-today life of slaves has been gleaned from oral histories passed from generation to generation rather than the written word. In *Slave Narratives from the Federal Writers Project, 1936–1938*, Dennis Simms, a slave from the Contee plantation in Laurel, Maryland, stated, "We were never allowed to congregate after work, never went to church, and could not read or write…we were kept in ignorance. We were unhappy." Simms also stated, "We lived in rudely constructed log houses, one story in height, with huge stone chimneys, and slept on beds of straw. In summer, the slaves went without shoes and wore three-quarter checkered baggy pants, some wearing only a long shirt to cover their body. Our food consisted of bread, hominy, black strap molasses and a red herring a day. Sometimes, by special permission from our master or overseer, we would go hunting and catch a coon or possum, and a pot pie would be a real treat."[156]

Life on the plantation tended to resemble that of a small or large village, depending on the size of the plantation and the rules and duties of the slaves. Some male slaves worked as skilled artisans and served as carpenters, shoemakers, blacksmiths, masons and/or tailors. Plantation records indicate that slave owners could and would rent out the services of these skilled slaves to others and pocket the wages for themselves. The work of a slave was also determined by the sex of the slave. Male slaves tended to work as field hands, skilled artisans, drivers or butlers. Female slaves might work in the field, but they could also serve the family as a cook, housemaid, nursemaid, and/or spinner. Life on a plantation might also include a slave hierarchy, with the house slaves who worked in the master's home being on the top of the chain, followed by those slaves who were skilled artisans in the middle and those who worked predominantly in the field at the bottom. This hierarchy could also be exhibited in the clothes worn by the slaves, with the house slaves clothed in nice, clean, crisp garments and the field slaves clothed in very rough, plain, rag-like clothes.[157]

Slaves constantly lived under the fear of punishment from their masters for either violating the Maryland slave code or not pleasing their slave master or overseer. In Maryland, slaves were not allowed to travel freely without a permit given by their master. According to Simms, "If a slave was caught beyond the limits of the plantation where he was employed, without the company of a white person or without written permit of his master, any person who apprehended him was permitted to give him twenty lashes across the bare back. Sometimes, Negro slave runaways who were apprehended by the patrollers, who kept a constant watch for escaped slaves, besides being flogged, would be branded with a hot iron on the cheek (or any other body part) with the letter 'R.'"[158] Any and all punishment was decided by the slave owner and defined by the State of Maryland. If slave master went too far in his punishment, he faced no recourse or punishment from the state.

FAMILY LIFE

It goes without saying that slaves, for the most part, did not enjoy the nuances of what is now perceived as a nuclear family—mother, father, children and other family members living under one roof. For one thing, slave marriages had no legal standing in the state of Maryland, as slaves were not married by church clergy. Instead, a majority of slave marriages included the slave ritual of "jumping the broom," in which the slave couple jumped over a broomstick at the same time to signify that there were married. It was also not uncommon for married slave couples to live and work on different plantations during the week and meet only during the weekends and/or special holidays. Despite any familial connections slaves might have felt toward each other, at the end of the day, slaves were considered to be personal property of the slave owner and as such could be sold. If a slave owner needed an infusion of money, the most worthwhile asset in his portfolio besides his land would be his slaves. The threat of being sold was a big fear for every slave family. If and when a slave master died, there was always the possibility that a slave could be willed to another family member who didn't live close by, or worse, didn't live in Maryland but rather farther south.

Nellie Saunders was a house servant at Three Sisters Plantation in Collington, Maryland. In 1841, she married Adam Plummer, a slave from the Riversdale plantation. At some point during their marriage, the couple planned to escape to Canada using their marriage license as free papers. Unfortunately, they were discovered when a family relative reported their escape plans to their owner. As punishment, Emily and several of her children were sold to another slaveholder, who did not live in Prince George's County but rather in Washington, D.C. Under existing Maryland law, children followed the status of their mother. Therefore, if the mother was a slave and the father a freed black, the children were considered slaves. A child born to parents who were free was no better off. As soon as the child had the ability to work or learn a trade, he needed to do so as soon as possible. If the parents failed to choose either option, then the child could find him or herself apprenticed to the Orphans Court, and the freed parents would have no recourse.

men, and the entire lot being young and
prime Servants.

All her stock of HORSES,
        MULES,
                CATTLE—among them several
                YOKES OF OXEN and
                MILCH COWS,
                HOGS, SHEEP,
                        All her Household and
Kitchen Furniture,
        Farming Implements,
                Several Wogons, Ox-Carts,
                | Corn, Oats and Provender,
                        A Lot of Good Pork,
                                Crop of Tobacco hanging in
the house, and the Crop of Wheat seeded
last fall.
        THE TERMS OF SALE ARE AS FOL-
LOWS:—The servants to be sold for cash or for
acceptances at six months at the election of the
purchaser, the interest added, to be approved by
the Administrator.

An 1858 announcement in the *Planter's Advocate* advertised a public sale of the estate of Mary Berry. Twenty-nine slaves were sold to several different owners. *Maryland State Archives.*

ABOLITIONISTS IN MARYLAND

It would be wrong to assume that a majority of the white population and the freed blacks of Maryland agreed with the practice of slavery or that many slaves were simply content with their lot in life. From the early days in the Maryland colony when blacks first arrived, as well as in the succeeding years that saw blacks made slaves for life, there were a growing number of people who believed that slavery was morally wrong. According to James M. McPherson, a Civil War historian, an abolitionist was defined as someone who, prior to the Civil War, believed in and fought for the immediate, unconditional and total abolition of slavery in the United States. Those in Maryland who called for the abolition of slavery in the state were of the opinion that the former slaves of Maryland should be returned to their homeland of Africa. Following Nat Turner's rebellion, the Maryland General Assembly again revised the state's manumission policy, allowing slave masters to free their slaves by will or deed with the provision that the slave leave the state of Maryland. This led some Marylanders to found the Maryland State Colonization Society in 1831, which advocated the return of freed blacks to Africa and led to the founding of Liberia. The Maryland legislature appropriated $200,000 to fund this endeavor for twenty years. The appropriation was renewed in 1852, with $10,000 allotted for six years, and in 1858, the appropriation was renewed for an additional four years with an annual payment of $5,000.[159] In 1860, the organization lost its funding.

In 1860, the manumission policy was again altered by the General Assembly as slave owners were prohibited from manumission by will and deed. Blacks who had previously been considered freed were now slaves. Blacks who were manumitted before the change in the law but still serving their terms were omitted from the 1860 law.[160] As the war drew to a close, the legislators repealed the previous legislation and allowed slave owners to free their slaves. At the same time, there was a significant number of whites who feared violence and retribution from the number of blacks—both freed and those held in bondage—in the state of Maryland. These fears came to realization not in Maryland but in Virginia. Led by John Brown in October 1859, a group of white and black abolitionists conducted a raid on Harpers Ferry, which was a Federal arms depot in Virginia. The original intent of the raid was to arm slaves, thus giving them the opportunity to fight for their freedom. While this raid was unsuccessful and led to the trial and execution of Brown and his followers, it did have a profound effect on some Maryland citizens. Curtis Jacobs, who represented Maryland's Eastern

Shore in the House of Delegates, introduced a bill that would have prevented Marylanders from freeing their slaves and, more importantly, forced all freed blacks to hire themselves out to whites on a permanent basis. While this bill passed the legislature, it failed to garner enough support when put to the vote to the people of Maryland. According to John Marck in *Maryland: The Seventh State*, although Marylanders before the Civil War were divided on the question of slavery, three prevailing opinions existed: some believed that owning slaves was wrong, others believed that it was wrong to make a slave of any man and still others believe that although they owned slaves, they should be freed when it was affordable to do so.[161]

THE UNDERGROUND RAILROAD

In *The Liberty Line: The Legend of the Underground Railroad*, Larry Gara notes that "the desire to purge the United States of what many perceived to be evil practice of slavery were blacks, both those who were slave and free, aided by white allies, who operated an illegal network determined to strike at slavery by helping those trapped in bondage." The blacks and whites were "conductors" for their slave "passengers" and "cargoes" who were given sanctuary in the homes and businesses that served as "stations" along the many escape routes. Those who participated in the Underground Railroad were hunted by the Federal government, disapproved of by the Northern majority and despised by the slaveholding South.[162] Called the "Moses of her People," Harriet Tubman, a former slave from Dorchester County, Maryland, was often associated with the Underground Railroad and led more than three hundred runaways to freedom. The slaves from Prince George's County who sought freedom through the Underground Railroad utilized an old Indian trial called the Georgetown Path, which ran north from Washington, D.C., and passed near Annapolis on to Baltimore and then Pennsylvania.[163] Or they may have traveled on the route that directed them to the Northwest Branch Creek from the Anacostia River to the town of Sandy Spring (Montgomery County), stopping in Laurel, Maryland, on the way to Baltimore before heading farther north.[164]

SLAVERY DURING THE CIVIL WAR

Before the war began, Prince George's County was home to the largest concentration of slaves in the state of Maryland. As the war raged on, due to Prince George's County's proximity to Washington, D.C., the scent of freedom was a lure to many slaves who ran to freedom by crossing over to the capital. In 1862, slavery was abolished in the District of Columbia. Beginning in 1863, male slaves were also given the option of joining the Federal army in exchange for their freedom. Some of these slaves were most likely a part of Company E, Fourth United States Colored Infantry, which was composed of freed African Americans as well as runaway slaves and was trained at Fort Lincoln, near Bladensburg. In 1863, Oden Bowie lost a reported seventy slaves who enlisted in the Union.[165] Dr. John H. Bayne, a respected physician who represented Prince George's County in the state legislature during the Civil War, would also play a role in advocating the return of all runaway slaves to all slave owners. A committee consisting of slave owners from Prince George's (including Dr. Bayne), Anne Arundel and Calvert Counties complained to Governor Bradford about the number of slaves escaping from respective counties and fleeing to Washington, D.C.

The committee requested that Governor Bradford establish armed forces to prevent the fleeing of slaves. While Bradford did not act on this suggestion, he did make an attempt to see President Lincoln to seek Federal assistance in capturing the runaways.

As the war progressed, it became apparent to those in power in the Maryland government that the institution of slavery needed to be abolished in the state. Events

Maryland governor Augustus Bradford.
Courtesy of Maryland State Archives.

that occurred outside of Prince George's County assisted in achieving this goal. In 1861, Congress passed the First Confiscation Act, which permitted court proceedings for the confiscation of any property, including slaves, being used to support the Confederate independence effort. The Fugitive Slave Act of 1850 was amended in 1862 to bar soldiers from aiding in the recapture of fugitives from disloyal masters. Likewise, the Second Confiscation Act of 1862 declared outright that fugitives of persons supporting the rebellion were free, regardless of the ex-slave's employment.[166] The U.S. Congress declared that compensation would be paid by the Federal government to slave owners who freed their slaves. Slavery was abolished in the District of Columbia on April 16, 1862, and slave owners were subsequently compensated.

The freeing of slaves in the District of Columbia had an immediate effect on slaves in Prince George's County. As the Federal city and the

Colored war contraband in the Civil War. *Library of Congress, Prints and Photographs Division.*

county shared boundaries, many slaves began escaping their plantations and seeking refuge in the District. The Second Confiscation Act also allowed the Union army to enlist blacks with the promise of freedom and barred using the Union army to recapture runaway slaves. President Lincoln also proposed to Congressman John Crisfield that the Federal government buy out Maryland slave owners by paying the owners $300 for each freed slave. Unfortunately for the Prince George's County slave owner, Congressman Crisfield of Kent County subsequently turned down the offer.[167] These events had a direct impact on slaves in Maryland who used the chaos created by war to run away from the plantations. Maryland slave owners appealed to Governor Thomas Bradford for assistance, and he in turn appealed to the Federal government to return fugitive slaves. There was also a growing number of slaves from Maryland who left their plantations and joined the Union army based on the promise of receiving their freedom in exchange for military service.

EMANCIPATION PROCLAMATION

Following the Battle of Antietam, President Lincoln outlined plans of the Emancipation Proclamation, which was to take effect on January 1, 1863. In essence, the Emancipation Proclamation freed slaves in the states that rebelled against the Union in addition to those that were currently occupied by Federal troops. As Maryland had never seceded from the Union, this proclamation had no immediate effect in Prince George's County. The Emancipation Proclamation was also in direct conflict with an existing Maryland law, which, as stated in Article 3, Section 42 of the Constitution of 1851, strictly forbade the passage of "any law abolishing the relation of master or slave, as it now exists in this State."[168]

The Emancipation Proclamation had freed the slaves in the rebelling Confederate states, and it was becoming harder and harder for the Union Party of Maryland to claim support for the Union and justify the continued existence of slavery in the state. Many Prince Georgian slave owners wanted the continuation of slavery in the county based on economic reasons (the loss of free labor) as well as social and moral reasons (they felt blacks were inferior to whites). As long as the war was fought to preserve the Union and not to end slavery, the Union Party held on to power in Prince George's County—at least until President Lincoln issued the Emancipation

President Abraham Lincoln and cabinet members at the first reading of the Emancipation Proclamation. *Library of Congress.*

Proclamation. Once the war was tied to ending slavery, the political power of the Union Party in Prince George's County took a negative hit.

An African American military service policy was established by the Maryland General Assembly in 1864. A law passed by the legislature awarded a bounty to slaveholders for enlisting their slaves in the Union effort. The act provided $100 to masters for enlisting their slaves, in addition to the $300 offered by the Federal government after a deed of manumission for the slaves. The enlisted slave received $50 once mustered into the military and another $50 when he was discharged. All Maryland slaves between the ages of eighteen and forty-five were required to be drafted.[169]

There were many who escaped slavery not by joining the Union army but by simply running away. Despite the Emancipation Proclamation, many blacks and whites were arrested and remanded by local officials for assisting runaway slaves. Charles Heise, a white man originally from South Carolina, was one of those people. Heise was convicted on November 17, 1863, of aiding in the escape of slaves Lethe, Louisa, Dick and Eveline from slaveholder William A. Talburtt. Charles Heise was sentenced to six years and six months in the Maryland State Penitentiary. Despite pleas from the government officials who presided over this trial, including the judge and state attorney, Heise was committed to the penitentiary on November 25. However, he was pardoned by Governor Bradford on December 15 and released from prison on December 16.[170]

MARYLAND CONSTITUTION OF 1864

On April 6, 1864, Edward W. Belt, Samuel H. Berry, Daniel Clarke and Fendall Marbury were elected to represent Prince George's County at the Constitutional Convention, which was held in Annapolis on April 27, 1864. The abolition of slavery in Maryland was a hotly debated topic among the delegates, including compensating their masters for the loss of their property. Dr. John H. Bayne of Prince George's County, who once sought assistance from Federal and state officials in the return of runaway slaves, had since reconciled himself with the abolition of slavery. Dr. Bayne argued, "Slavery has militated against the development of the resources and prosperity of the state." In addition to believing that slavery was morally wrong, many legislators believed that the commerce, internal improvements, agriculture and industry would improve with emancipation.[171] In addition, pardons for slave code offenders and the right to regulate freed blacks for representation in the House of Delegates were important points of contention. The constitution also disenfranchised those who supported the Confederacy and altered the legislative makeup of the Maryland General Assembly. On October 13, 1864, the constitution was ratified by a vote of 30,174–29,799 in an election marred by allegations of voter intimidation and voting irregularities.[172] In addition, the composition of the Maryland General Assembly was altered to limit the power of the smaller counties that previously had large populations of slaves. In November 1864, the Constitution of 1864 became the law of Maryland. While the institution of slavery was over, its lasting effects would reverberate in the county for the next one hundred years. For many slaves such as the Plummer family, emancipation was neither political nor an economic act; it was simply a humane act that freed them from the curse of slavery. As Nellie Arnold Plummer said, "O, how fervently they did praise the Lord for their deliverance from slavery!"[173]

Conclusion

The Civil War came to an end on April 9, 1865, when Confederate general Robert E. Lee surrendered to Union general Ulysses S. Grant at Appomattox Court House in Virginia. The conclusion of the war found both sides trying to rebound both financially and socially, and Prince George's County was in total disarray. Many of the landowners found themselves bankrupt and in possession of worthless Confederate bonds, and those who were unable to meet the taxes assessed by the Federal government lost their farms.[174] Many of the returning veterans were not in any condition physically or emotionally to farm their land without the benefit of slave labor. The county also had to adjust to a population of freed slaves, who found themselves trying to adjust to a new life in Prince George's County. Many of the former slaves left the county following the war. The farms that did manage to remain intact now found themselves dealing with the loss of their free labor.

The abolishment of slavery led to new dynamic for both the black and white citizens of Prince George's County as the former slaves adjusted to freedom and the whites adjusted to a free black population. Despite the passage of the Thirteenth Amendment, which outlawed slavery in the United States, the State of Maryland rejected the subsequent Fourteenth Amendment, which granted former slaves citizenship, and the Fifteenth Amendment, which gave former male slaves the right to vote. Despite these rejections, both amendments were later approved by a majority of the states. Following Reconstruction, the white population attempted to control the black population of Prince George's County with sharecropping contracts and Jim Crow laws that separated the races in regards to education and public facilities. The Freedmen's Bureau was established by the federal government to help the former slaves by assisting with changing the marital status, serving as a negotiator between the former slave owners and slaves and creating new schools for the freed blacks. In 1865, there were 43 primary schools. By 1885, there were 65, and by 1908, there were 112—73 white and 39 black.[175]

In the years following the war, the population of the county grew as Prince George's became home to new immigrants. The white population of the county nearly doubled from ten thousand in 1860 to eighteen thousand in 1900. By 1870, 30 percent of the black population had left Prince George's County, but by 1880, the number of blacks in the county had increased to almost prewar levels. Following the conclusion of the war, many large plantations became small farms. As a result, the number of farms increased from 800 in 1870 to 2,400 in 1900, with the average size of farms decreasing. In 1880, the average farm was 159 acres; that number had decreased to 142 acres in 1890 and 111 acres in 1900.[176] The agricultural economy was rebounding as well. Although the production of tobacco didn't immediately rebound to its prewar levels, by 1880, tobacco production in the county was 6 million pounds. As the twenty-first century began, the old Prince George's that existed prior to the Civil War was no more.

Notes

Introduction

1. Students of History 429, *Knowing Our History*.

Chapter 1

2. Detwiler, *Bicycling Through Civil War History*.
3. Chappelle et al, *Maryland: A History of Its People*.

Chapter 2

4. Cox, *Civil War Maryland*.

Chapter 3

5. Virta, "Graveyard of Prince George's County," 2.
6. Baker et al, *Battle Lines*.
7. Virta, "Graveyard of Prince George's County," 2.
8. Ibid.
9. Virta, *Prince George's County*, 121.
10. Ibid., 122.
11. U.S. National Park Service, "Fort Foote Park: History & Culture."
12. Ibid., "Fort Washington: History & Culture."
13. Salay, "'Very Picturesque, But Regarded as Nearly Useless,'" 67–86.
14. U.S. National Park Service, "Fort Washington: History & Culture."

15. Ibid.
16. Salay, "'Very Picturesque, But Regarded as Nearly Useless,'" 67–86.
17. Ibid.
18. U.S. National Park Service, "Fort Washington: History & Culture."
19. Salay, "'Very Picturesque, But Regarded as Nearly Useless,'" 67–86.
20. U.S. National Park Service, "Fort Foote Park: History & Culture."
21. Ibid.
22. Ibid., "Fort Foote."
23. Ibid., "Fort Washington: History & Culture."
24. Virta, "Graveyard of Prince George's County," 2.
25. U.S. National Park Service, "Fort Foote Park: History & Culture."
26. Mahan, *A Treatise on Field Fortification*, 17.
27. U.S. National Park Service, "The Marvel of the Big Guns at Fort Foote."
28. Ibid., "Fort Foote."
29. Ibid., "Fort Foote Park: History & Culture."
30. Ibid.
31. Ibid.
32. Ibid.
33. Ibid.
34. Roe, *The Ninth New York Heavy Artillery*.
35. U.S. National Park Service, "Fort Foote Park: History & Culture."
36. Ibid.
37. Roe, *The Ninth New York Heavy Artillery.*
38. U.S. National Park Service, "The Marvel of the Big Guns at Fort Foote."
39. Ibid., "Fort Foote Park: History & Culture."
40. Ibid., "The Marvel of the Big Guns at Fort Foote."
41. Maryland Inventory of Historic Properties, "Fort Lincoln Cemetery."
42. U.S. National Park Service, "Civil War Defenses of Washington: Appendix C: Naming the Forts."
43. Maryland Inventory of Historic Properties, "Fort Lincoln Cemetery."
44. Ibid.
45. *Maryland Courier*, "Fort Lincoln Cemetery."
46. Virta, *Prince George's County*, 128.
47. Baker et al, *Battle Lines*.
48. Virta, *Prince George's County*, 122.
49. Baker et al, *Battle Lines*.
50. Ibid.
51. Ibid.
52. Ibid.
53. U.S. Government Printing Office, *Fort Washington*.
54. U.S. National Park Service, "Fort Foote Park: History & Culture."
55. Ibid.
56. Ibid.

CHAPTER 4

57. Chapelle et al, *Maryland: A History of Its People.*
58. Walsh and Fox, *Maryland.*
59. Virta, *Prince George's County.*
60. Message from the governor to the General Assembly, http://www.archive.org/stream/messageofgoverno1860hick/messageofgoverno1860hick_djvu.txt.
61. Maryland State Archives, "Thomas Holliday Hicks." http://msa.maryland.gov/megafile/msa/speccol/sc3500/sc3520/001400/001462/html/1462extbio.html.
62. Walsh and Fox, Maryland.
63. Chappelle et al, *Maryland: A History of Its People.*
64. Ibid.
65. Maryland State Archives, "Civil War and the Maryland General Assembly."
66. Newman, *Maryland and the Confederacy.*
67. Ibid.
68. Ibid.
69. Ibid.
70. Virta, *Prince George's County.*
71. Newman, *Maryland and the Confederacy.*
72. Ibid.
73. Ibid.
74. Ibid.
75. Dave Leip's Atlas on Presidential Elections, "1864 Presidential Election Results."
76. Newman, *Maryland and the Confederacy.*

CHAPTER 5

77. Watson, *Prince George's County*, 44.
78. Maryland-National Capital Parks and Planning Commission, "Surratt House Museum."
79. Virta, *Prince George's County*, 120.
80. Baker et al, *Battle Lines.*
81. Virta, *Prince George's County*, 120.
82. Watson, *Prince George's County*, 44.
83. Baker et al, *Battle Lines.*
84. Virta, *Prince George's County*, 120.
85. Ibid., 124.
86. Watson, *Prince George's County*, 44.
87. Virta, *Prince George's County*, 124.
88. Maryland State Archives Special Collections, "*Marlboro Gazette* and *Prince George's Advertiser* Collection."
89. Turner, *The Planters' Advocate*, November 12, 1851.
90. Ibid., June 19, 1861.
91. Ibid.
92. Maryland State Archives Special Collections, "Planter's Advocate Collection."

93. Virta, *Prince George's County*, 120.

94. Baker et al, *Battle Lines*.

95. Ibid.

96. Watson, *Prince George's County*, 44.

97. Ibid.

98. Toomey, *The Civil War in Maryland*, 149.

99. Maryland Civil War Centennial Commission, "Maryland Remembers," 35.

100. Baker et al, *Battle Lines*.

101. Verge, *Between the Lines*.

102. Baker et al, *Battle Lines*.

103. Newman, *Maryland and the Confederacy*, 76.

104. Verge, *Between the Lines*.

105. Newman, *Maryland and the Confederacy*, 76.

106. Baker et al, *Battle Lines*.

107. Ibid.

108. Leonard, *Lincoln's Avengers*, 43.

109. Ibid.

110. Larson, *The Assassin's Accomplice*, 12.

111. Trindal, *Mary Surratt*, 20, 22.

112. Larson, Kate Clifford. *The Assassin's Accomplice*, 14.

113. Maryland-National Capital Parks and Planning Commission, "Surratt House Museum."

114. Ibid.

115. Baker et al, *Battle Lines*.

116. Maryland-National Capital Parks and Planning Commission, "Surratt House Museum."

117. Baker et al, *Battle Lines*.

118. Maryland-National Capital Parks and Planning Commission, "Surratt House Museum."

119. Baker et al, *Battle Lines*.

120. Maryland-National Capital Parks and Planning Commission, "Surratt House Museum."

121. Baker et al, *Battle Lines*.

122. Maryland-National Capital Parks and Planning Commission, "Surratt House Museum."

123. Isacsson, "John Surratt and the Lincoln Assassination Plot," 318.

124. Maryland-National Capital Parks and Planning Commission, "Surratt House Museum."

125. Ibid.

126. Baker et al, *Battle Lines*.

127. Isacsson, "John Surratt and the Lincoln Assassination Plot," 318.

128. Donald, *Lincoln*, 588.

129. Baker et al, *Battle Lines*.

130. Maryland-National Capital Parks and Planning Commission, "Surratt House Museum."

131. Baker et al, *Battle Lines*.

132. Maryland Civil War Centennial Commission, "Maryland Remembers," 35.

133. Maryland-National Capital Parks and Planning Commission, "Surratt House Museum."

134. Ibid.

135. Ward, *The Civil War*, 361–63.

136. Maryland Civil War Centennial Commission, "Maryland Remembers," 35.

137. Maryland-National Capital Parks and Planning Commission, "Surratt House Museum."

138. Larson, *The Assassin's Accomplice*, 77.

139. Farquhar, "The Haunting Tale of Mary Surratt."

140. Baker et al, *Battle Lines*.

141. Maryland-National Capital Parks and Planning Commission, "Surratt House Museum."

142. George, "The Trials of John H. Surratt," 17.

143. Isacsson, "John Surratt and the Lincoln Assassination Plot," 318.

144. George, "The Trials of John H. Surratt," 17.

CHAPTER 6

145. Mills, *"Got My Mind Set on Freedom."*

146. Maryland State Archives, "Blacks Before the Law in Colonial Maryland."

147. Rollo, *The Black Experience in Maryland*.

148. Mills, *"Got My Mind Set on Freedom."*

149. Wright, *The Free Negro in Maryland*.

150. Ibid.

151. Chappelle et al, *Maryland: A History of Its People*.

152. Switala, *Underground Railroad*.

153. Mills, *"Got My Mind Set on Freedom."*

154. Geiger, *Maryland Our Maryland*.

155. Davis, *Slavery in the Colonial Chesapeake*.

156. Federal Writers Project, *Maryland Slave Narratives*.

157. Rollo, *The Black Experience In Maryland*.

158. Federal Writers Project, *Maryland Slave Narratives*.

159. Guy, *Maryland's Persistent Pursuit to End Slavery*.

160. Ibid.

161. Marck, *Maryland: The Seventh State*.

162. Gara, *The Liberty Line*.

163. Ibid.

164. Switala, *Underground Railroad*.

165. Virta, *Prince George's County*.

166. Whitman, *Challenging Slavery in the Chesapeake*.

167. Rhodes, *Somerset County, Maryland*.

168. Maryland State Archives, "Constitutional Convention of 1864."

169. Guy, *Maryland's Persistent Pursuit to End Slavery*.

170. Maryland State Archives, "Charles Heise."
171. Guy, *Maryland's Persistent Pursuit to End Slavery*.
172. Cox, *Civil War Maryland*.
173. Virta, *Prince George's County*.

Conclusion

174. Newman, *Maryland and the Confederacy*.
175. Virta, *Prince George's County*.
176. Ibid.

Bibliography

Periodicals

Farquhar, Michael. "The Haunting Tale of Mary Surratt." *Washington Post*, October 31, 1991.

George, Joseph, Jr. "The Trials of John H. Surratt." *Maryland Historical Magazine* 99, no. 1 (2004).

Isacsson, Alfred. "John Surratt and the Lincoln Assassination Plot." *Maryland Historical Magazine* 52, no. 4 (December 1957).

Maryland Courier. "Fort Lincoln Cemetery." March 1977.

Salay, David L. "'Very Picturesque, But Regarded as Nearly Useless': Fort Washington, Maryland, 1816–1872." *Maryland Historical Magazine* 81, no. 1 (1986).

Turner, Thomas J. *The Planters' Advocate*. November 12, 1851, and June 19, 1861.

Virta, Alan. "Graveyard of Prince George's County." *News and Notes from the Prince George's County Historical Society* 6, no. 9 (September 1972).

Books

Baker, Lindsay, Mary Jurkiewicz, Aaron Marcavitch and Laurie Verge. *Battle Lines: Prince George's County in the Civil War*. Upper Marlboro, MD: Prince George's County History Consortium, 2011.

Bowie, Effie Gwynn. *Across the Years in Prince George's County*. Baltimore, MD: Genealogical Publishing, 1947.

Callum, Agnes K. *Colored Volunteers of the Maryland Civil War: 7th Regiment, United States Color Troops, 1863–1866*. Baltimore, MD: Mullac Publishers, 1990.

Campbell, Helen Jones. *The Case for Mrs. Surratt*. New York: G.P. Putnam's Sons, 1943.

Chappelle, Suzanne E., Jean H. Baker, Dean R. Esslinger, Whitman H. Ridgway, Constance B. Schulz and Gregory A. Stiverson. *Maryland: A History of Its People.* Baltimore, MD: Johns Hopkins University Press, 1986.

Cox, Richard P. *Civil War Maryland: Stories from the Old Line State.* Charleston, SC: The History Press, 2008.

Davis, David B. *Slavery in the Colonial Chesapeake.* Williamsburg, VA: Colonial Williamsburg Foundation, 1986.

Detwiler, Kurt B. *Bicycling through Civil War History.* Mclean, VA: EPM Publications, 1994.

Donald, David Herbert. *Lincoln.* New York: Simon & Schuster, 1995.

Federal Writers Project. *Maryland Slave Narratives.* Carlisle, MA: Applewood Books, 2006.

Fields, Barbara. *Slavery and Freedom on the Middle Ground: Maryland During the 19th Century.* New Haven, CT: Yale University Press, 1958.

Gara, Larry. *The Liberty Line: The Legend of the Underground Railroad.* Lexington: University Press of Kentucky, 1996.

Geiger, Virginia, ed. *Maryland Our Maryland.* Lanham, MD: United Press of America Inc., 1987.

Guy, Anita G. *Maryland's Persistent Pursuit to End Slavery, 1850–1864.* New York: Garland Publishing Inc., 1997.

Hartzler, Daniel D. *Marylanders in the Confederacy.* Silver Spring, MD: Family Line Publications, 1986.

Larson, Kate Clifford. *The Assassin's Accomplice: Mary Surratt and the Plot to Kill Abraham Lincoln.* New York: Basic Books, 2008.

Leonard, Elizabeth D. *Lincoln's Avengers: Justice, Revenge, and Reunion After the Civil War.* New York: Norton, 2004.

Mahan, Dennis Hart. *A Treatise on Field Fortification: Containing Instructions on the Method of Laying Out, Constructing, Defending, and Attacking Intrenchments, with the General Outlines Also of the Arrangement, the Attack, and Defence of Permanent Fortifications.* New York: John Wiley, 1863.

Manakee, Harold R. *Maryland in the Civil War.* Baltimore: Maryland Historical Society, 1961.

Marck, John T. *Maryland: The Seventh State: A History.* New York: Creative Impressions, 1993.

Maryland Civil War Centennial Commission. "Maryland Remembers: A Guide to Historic Places and People of the Civil War in Maryland." Hagerstown, MD: 1961.

Maryland Inventory of Historic Properties. "Fort Lincoln Cemetery." Crownsville, MD: Maryland Historical Trust, 1998.

Mills, Barbara. *"Got My Mind Set on Freedom": Maryland's Story of Black and White Activism, 1663–2000.* Baltimore, MD: Heritage Books Inc., 2002.

Mitchell, Charles, W. *Maryland Voices of the Civil War.* Baltimore, MD: Johns Hopkins University Press, 2007.

Moore, L. Tilden. *1890 Special Census of the Civil War Veterans of the State of Maryland, Vol. II: Carroll, Frederick, Montgomery, Prince George's, Calvert, Charles and St. Mary's Counties.* Westminster, MD: Willow Bend Books, 2001.

Newman, Harry Wright. *Maryland and the Confederacy: An Objective Narrative of Maryland's Participation in the War Between the States, 1861–1865.* Annapolis, MD: Newman, 1976.

Rhodes, Jason. *Somerset County, Maryland: A Brief History*. Charleston, SC: The History Press, 2007.

Riley, Elihu S. *A History of the General Assembly of Maryland, 1635–1904*. Baltimore, MD: Nunn & Co., 1904.

———. *Message of the Governor of Maryland to the General Assembly in Extra Session, 1861*. Frederick, MD: E.S. Riley , 1861.

Roe, Alfred Seelye. *The Ninth New York Heavy Artillery*. Worcester, MD: self-published, 1899.

Rollo, Vera F. *The Black Experience in Maryland*. Lanham: Maryland Historical Press, 1984.

Ruffner, Kevin Conley. *Maryland's Blue & Gray: A Border State's Union and Confederate Junior Officer Corps*. Baton Rouge: Louisiana State University Press, 1997.

Students of History 429. *Knowing Our History: African American Slavery and the University of Maryland*. College Park: University of Maryland, 2009.

Switala, William J. *Underground Railroad in Delaware, Maryland and West Virginia*. Mechanicsburg, PA: Stackpole Books, 2004.

Thornton, Alvin, PhD, Karen Williams Gooden and Bianca Floyd. *Like a Phoenix I'll Rise: An Illustrated History of African Americans in Prince George's County, Maryland, 1696–1996*. Virginia Beach, VA: Donning Company, 1997.

Toomey, Daniel Carroll. *The Civil War in Maryland*. Baltimore, MD: Toomey Press, 1983.

Trindal, Elizabeth Steger. *Mary Surratt: An American Tragedy*. Gretna, LA: Pelican Publishing Co., 1996.

U.S. Government Printing Office. *Fort Washington*. Washington, D.C.: 1952.

Verge, Laurie. *Between the Lines: Southern Maryland and the Civil War*. Clinton, MD: Surratt House Museum, 2012.

Virta, Alan. *Prince George's County: A Pictorial History*. Virginia Beach, VA: Donning Company, 1984.

Walsh, Richard, and William Lloyd Fox. *Maryland: A History, 1632–1974*. Baltimore: Maryland Historical Society, 1974.

Ward, Geoffrey C. *The Civil War: An Illustrated History*. New York: Alfred A. Knopf, 1990.

Watson, James Douglas. *Prince George's County: Past and Present*. Washington, D.C.: Federal Lithograph Co., 1962.

Whitman, T. Stephen. *Challenging Slavery in the Chesapeake: Black and White Resistance to Human Bondage, 1775–1865*. Baltimore: Maryland Historical Society, 2006.

Wright, James. *The Free Negro in Maryland, 1634–1860*. Whitefish, MT: Kessinger Publishing Reprints, 2010.

WEBSITES

Anacostia Community Museum. "Adam Plummer Teaching Documents." http://anacostia.si.edu/Plummer/Docs/Teacher_Resources/High_School/hsslaveryreading.pdf.

Dave Leip's Atlas on Presidential Elections. "1864 Presidential Election Results." http://uselectionatlas.org/RESULTS/data.php?year=1864&datatype=national&def=1&f=0&off=0&elect=0.

Maryland-National Capital Parks and Planning Commission. "Surratt House Museum." http://www.pgparks.com/places/eleganthistoric/surratt_history.html.

Maryland State Archives. "Augustus W. Bradford (1806–1881)." http://msa.maryland.gov/megafile/msa/speccol/sc3500/sc3520/001400/001463/html/1463bio2.html.

———. "Blacks Before the Law in Colonial Maryland." http://msa.maryland.gov/msa/speccol/sc5300/sc5348/html/chap3.html.

———. "Charles Heise." http://msa.maryland.gov/megafile/msa/speccol/sc5400/sc5496/003300/003396/html/003396bio.html.

———. "Civil War and the Maryland General Assembly." http://msa.maryland.gov/msa/stagser/s1259/121/7590/html/0000.html.

———. "Constitutional Convention of 1864." http://msa.maryland.gov/msa/speccol/sc2600/sc2685/html/conv1864.html.

———. "Thomas Holliday Hicks (1798–1865). http://msa.maryland.gov/megafile/msa/speccol/sc3500/sc3520/001400/001462/html/1462extbio.html.

Maryland State Archives Special Collections. "*Marlboro Gazette* and *Prince George's Advertiser* Collection." http://speccol.mdarchives.state.md.us/msa/speccol/catalog/cfm/dsp_number.cfm.

———. "Planter's Advocate Collection." http://speccol.mdarchives.state.md.us/msa/speccol/catalog/cfm/dsp_number.cfm.

U.S. National Park Service. "Civil War Defenses of Washington: Appendix C: Naming the Forts." http://www.nps.gov/history/history/online_books/civilwar/hrsa1-c.htm.

———. "Fort Foote." http://www.nps.gov/cwdw/historyculture/fort-foote.htm.

———. "Fort Foote Park: History & Culture." http://www.nps.gov/fofo/historyculture/index.html.

———. "Fort Washington: History & Culture." http://www.nps.gov/fowa/historyculture/index.htm.

———. "The Marvel of the Big Guns at Fort Foote." http://www.nps.gov/cwdw/historyculture/the-marvel-of-the-big-guns-at-fort-foote.htm.

Index

About the Authors

From left to right: Nathania A. Branch Miles, Ryan J. Quick and Monday M. Miles.

MONDAY M. MILES is a graduate of the University of Maryland, College Park, with a bachelor's degree in history. She also has a master's degree from Trinity Washington University in nonprofit management/human resources management. She lives in Bowie, Maryland.

NATHANIA A. BRANCH MILES is a graduate of the University of Maryland, College Park, with a bachelor's degree in urban and regional planning. She is the coauthor of three books on the history of Prince George's County and an active member of several genealogical, historical and community organizations. She lives in Hyattsville, Maryland.

RYAN J. QUICK is a graduate of the University of Maryland, College Park, with a bachelor's degree in journalism and a minor in creative writing. He has worked as a news reporter and book editor. He lives in Greenbelt, Maryland.